BASEBALL

A Cricketer's Guide

◇

FRANCIS GLADSTONE

With a foreword by Peter Ueberroth
Commissioner for Baseball

THE KINGSWOOD PRESS

for
Willie and Pete

The Kingswood Press
an imprint of William Heinemann Ltd.
10 Upper Grosvenor Street, London W1X 9PA
LONDON   MELBOURNE
JOHANNESBURG   AUCKLAND

First published 1987
ISBN 0 434 98068 4

Photoset by Rowland Phototypesetting Ltd,
Bury St Edmunds, Suffolk
Printed and bound in Great Britain by
Butler & Tanner Ltd., Frome and London

CONTENTS

◇

FOREWORD

◇

Baseball, A Cricketer's Guide is a thoughtfully written guide for the spectator who is new or relatively new to the game. In careful and precise language, the author, Francis Gladstone, helps simplify a game that at first sight may seem intricate and complicated, if not downright mysterious.

Baseball, as the national pastime of the United States, has for more than one hundred years helped strengthen the fabric and moral fibre of our country. It has provided its fans with heroes and villains, with drama, with laughter and with sadness. It has also provided us with tradition, continuity, and, in times of difficulty, a strong sense of order.

It is a common bond that brings together family and friends, and often serves as a vehicle in establishing instant contact among strangers. Today, baseball is reaching out beyond the Americas, to Europe, to Africa, to Asia, Australia, the Pacific and establishing instant and friendly contact.

The game's popularity is increasing steadily and books such as Francis Gladstone's will help facilitate understanding about the game and initiate friendly contact among those who enjoy it.

Peter V. Ueberroth
New York City

February, 1987

AUTHOR'S NOTE

◇

American football has clearly caught on in Britain, and the fact that it has done so so quickly says a good deal about the power of television, and something about the way in which fewer and fewer sports are confined to their countries of origin.

And now that this has happened to American football, could it happen to baseball, not only in Britain, but in other cricketing countries?

It is too early to answer that question, but less early than when Derek Wyatt commissioned this book, in May 1986, about a game almost no one in Britain had seen, at least no one in the sense of mass television audiences. Baseball here has always had a small but significant number of devotees playing it at a very decent amateur level, particularly in the north. But then, just as this manuscript was being finished, three million people were watching the final of the World Series on Channel Four Television. Baseball suddenly seemed less of a curiosity to cricketing eyes.

But in spite of the size of the audience, it is a fact that baseball is not such an easy game to pick up as American Football. It has less obvious spectacle and – like cricket – the enjoyment of it comes from understanding a good deal about tactics and sides and individual players. You watch baseball not just for the moment, but the for moment in relation to past moments, involving a knowledge of averages and the kind of numerical gilding that makes the lily of cricket so attractive.

And cricketers – do not stop reading here. Inadequate as my explanation of baseball may be, it is the explanation of a cricket fan. Iconoclast, you may say, traitor, worshipper of brazen images. Perhaps; but just as religions, or different branches of religion, have common origins, and as a knowledge of one can be enlightening to a worshipper of the other, so these two small-ball games, baseball and cricket, seem to have the same roots. They also, I would suggest, have in common that they are games which touch their national characters more intimately, or at least as intimately, as football. Certainly in the US football has a more recent history, and has never aspired to being dubbed 'the (American) national pastime'. That honour is reserved for baseball.

As far as help with this book goes, my son Elwyn, as I explain, was the catalyst in the reaction that enabled me, at least to learn to love baseball. Thirteen years of American life constituted the medium in which the reaction took place; the other ingredients were many hours spent at Fenway Park in Boston, and glued to games on the box. I also want to thank specifically those American friends who gave me detailed help with this manuscript. It is not an easy task to explain a whole game, particularly one with all the ramifications of baseball. I wish I had done it better.

◇ 1 ◇

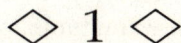

INITIATION ON A SNOWY DAY

And though this is certainly not the time or place to ask, there is a part of me . . . which still asks, Why this baseball?, Why not Greek tragedies or symphonies? Why not economics, history or philosophy?
Howard Senzel, baseball writer

There are runners at first and third bases and only one man out. Boston are behind four to three and it is the last part of the ninth inning. If they score one they will tie, and the game will go on for more innings until there is a result. If they score more than one, they will win. Jim Rice, who is a big hitter, comes into bat.

The first pitch from New York is wild, what is called a 'ball'. Rice lets it go. But the next one is straight and he hits it, low and hard, only to be caught at third base. Two out for Boston now. One more man out and they will be finished.

The next man comes in to bat, swings at a straight pitch and misses. One strike. The same thing, he swings and misses again. Two strikes. The next ball is straight too. But this time he hits it, high and deep, so deep into the field it may go out. The man at bat runs like hell to first base, the man on first base goes to second, the man on third runs for the home plate. This

1

last man gets there – that is the tying run – and as he does the ball slams into the wall on the far side of the ground.

As the fielder tries to grab it on the bounce back, the runner at second keeps on going to third. The crowd is now standing and cheering and, as he nears third base, we see that the fielder has misjudged the bounce and fumbles. The runner goes on. The fielder recovers, picks up the ball and hurls it to the catcher, the man at home plate. Like a diver at the pool the runner throws himself at the plate and reaches it at exactly the moment the catcher fields the ball. At least it seems that way to the spectator's eyes. But the umpire puts his right arm out horizontally and declares that the man is out. The runner picks himself up out of the sand and as he begins to quarrel with the umpire, who is a huge man in a blue jacket, the coach comes running on from the dugout. He too starts yelling at the umpire, and the crowd starts cheering, twenty five thousand voices, but the umpire will have none of it.

Had the man been home, Boston would have won, five to four. As it is they are even and this man out is their third for the inning, which is all that they are allowed. The game will now have to go on until there is a result.

This is the kind of climax – or potential climax – that you get from time to time in baseball. For at best baseball is a game in which the odds keep switching every few minutes through the roughly three and a half hours it takes to complete a game. Like cricket there is a lot of mind as well as matter in the game. Enjoying it depends as much on what you know about the sides, the players, the tactics, who pitches in a particular way, who is strong against whom, than in just looking at the hits. Indeed if you look at baseball for spectacle alone, without some inside knowledge you are likely to be as bored as an American at a cricket match. This is so much so that it could be said that the pleasure of baseball depends more on antici-pation than on events themselves. As in cricket what the bowler and the field are up to in terms of strategy is not

obvious to a first time viewer. As in cricket there is a great deal of language and jargon attached to the game, 'strike out', 'fielder's choice', 'bunting' and 'stealing', 'double play' and 'triple play', 'foul pop' and 'dead ball', 'slider' and 'knuckle ball'.

In the autumn – 'fall' in American English – of 1978, I knew none of this. My son Elwyn was five, going on six. He had a rudimentary collection of baseball cards, a Boston Red Sox hat, a Boston Red Sox souvenir book, a Boston Red Sox team poster, a fielder's glove, a small size ball and a small size bat. He watched baseball on television and asked me to take him to a professional game. I did this more as a duty than a pleasure and the pleasure was spoilt for both of us by the fact that a friend he took wanted to spend the whole game in the souvenir shop, then got bored and homesick. Elwyn was embarrassed by this. I assumed that the outing was not a great success and thought little more of it for a few weeks. Then I noticed that even out of season Elwyn began to read books about baseball and to leaf through the souvenir programme of the game we had seen. But when the long Massachusetts winter came he kept niggling me to take him to another game early in the next season. For baseball is like an addiction to nicotine. Once children in America have tried it they cannot forget. It is pulsing in the blood. In February and March the teams start spring training in the southern states, and Elwyn was already watching their progress in the *Boston Globe*. In April the season begins.

April weather in Boston can be almost anything. April 1979 was pretty bleak, and having refused to go to about four games, I eventually succumbed. I was not that busy. I was not away from home. We did not have visitors. There were no excuses. The majority of baseball games are played under lights, starting at 7.35 p.m. and ending around 11 o'clock, but he had found an afternoon game so that I could not claim late bedtime in the school term as an excuse. Perhaps the game we went to would be so boring that he would not want to go to

4

any more. After all baseball was a very boring game, and once he grew out of wanting Red Sox caps and bats he would probably see sense and forget all about it.

Boston were playing Texas and it was snowing, not hard, just swirls drifting in on a bitter north-east wind blowing across the roofs of the city to the ballpark via the coast of Maine and the Arctic Circle. The players, particularly the Texans, looked frozen. There was only a handful of spectators in the crowd – they too looked frozen, and so did I. Although I had taken the paper, somehow you can't read in a sports arena when there is something going on in front of you, particularly if you have to spend a lot of time stopping the wind penetrating the bottom of your trouser legs or the top of your scarf. For a reason that was still not clear to me, Elwyn did not seem frozen.

As far as I could see nothing much happened. The game the year before had been slow. This one was at a snail's pace. Occasionally someone would hit the ball, but not very often and generally when they did it was caught by the other side. Occasionally a foul ball would land in the crowd, a moment of some excitement because whoever catches the ball can keep it. But it never came very near us, something I felt quite glad about, for it seemed to move like a bullet. At the end of the game the score was one to nothing, a slim Boston victory. I was relieved. The game had been so bleak and boring that the boy must give up his addiction now.

But as we walked back to the ancient Boston underground, Elwyn kept asking questions: What did I think of the Texas pitcher? Did I think Boggs would keep hitting above four hundred? Did I think Boston was right to bring in a left handed pitcher in the eighth inning? Did I think that so and so would keep playing short stop? When could we go to another game? Could we go on a Friday evening as there was no school on Saturday? Or on Saturday? Or on Sunday? There was a 'double-header' on Sunday, he said, two games for the price of one played consecutively. I evaded a direct answer and said something about other commitments. We waited silently for the subway train to arrive.

It was crowded and there was little heat, but in spite of the jolting and the cold, I noticed that Elwyn was absorbed in the game programme, working out some average in his head. That, I think, was the moment of revelation. For I then realized that no amount of excuses would keep me from taking him to more games, and that if a six-year old could enjoy baseball in spite of bitter winds and little action, then so possibly could a forty-year old. Clearly those who go out for a smoke in the snow are badly addicted, and clearly this boy was getting a pleasure that I was missing. Thus began a commitment to go courting, with Elwyn as my chaperone. At first the courting was difficult, but soon I was in love and putting up with all the disappointments of intimacy, putting up with them because, for all its faults, baseball is a wonderful, active and intricate game. The first principle of baseball is that to enjoy it, you have to get inside it. At least that has been my experience in the years since that bitterly cold April day.

And really it was not that much different from my experience of cricket when I was a boy fan of the great Surrey teams of the early fifties, and in fantasy life was fielding in the slips for one of the Bedsers or Jim Laker, and being patted on the back by P. B. H. May as I made my heroic, diving, climactic catch and saved the game. How often had I dreamed of myself as one day having a small place in the Wisden I knew so well.

◇ 2 ◇

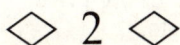

ABSOLUTE BEGINNINGS

Osteen hit two out, Maloney one, and that was the
score 2–1. The wind, blowing from left field, ham-
pered our right-handed power. The Fox had forgotten his buggy whip.

Jim Brosnan, Pennant Race

What follows are some brief notes on the absolute basics of
the game, the first step in learning the language. As any game
is difficult to learn except by watching it, everything in this
brief chapter is developed in the next chapter in a match
commentary. If you do not like learning basics, then skip on
to the chapter that follows.

As a starting point, a baseball field looks like this (see
diagram on p. 9).

THE FIELD AND THE FIELDERS

Most of the game takes place in the infield, which is defined by
the four bases making a diamond shape. These four bases are
called home plate at the bottom of the diamond, and then
moving right (or anti-clockwise) first base, second base and
third base. The man 'at bat', the hitter, stands in a box at

7

home plate. The pitcher faces him on the mound which is slightly raised. When he pitches one foot must stay on the pitcher's plate, or 'rubber' as it is known, which is twenty-four inches long and six inches wide. It is placed sixty and a half feet away from the home plate.

In the diagram, the shaded parts of the field are of sand, except for the bases and home plate which are pads anchored into the ground. The rest of the ground is either grass or astroturf. The area beyond the bases is called the outfield.

There are three outfielders: left field, centre field and right field. And there are four infielders: first base, second base, short stop and third base. Then there is the catcher behind home plate.

FOUL LINES AND BOUNDARIES

The foul lines run up the side of the field from home plate in a 'V' shape, the left foul line through third base to the boundary, the right foul line through first base. Each is not necessarily the same length as the other, because each baseball field has slightly different dimensions in the outfield. Thus in one field the right foul line may be three hundred and ten feet long and the left three hundred and thirty; in another they may run the same distance from home plate. And the arc of the boundary can vary in shape or can be irregular.

The reason for this is historical. The older grounds were built within existing streets and tram lines. Newer ones have depended on the management of the team involved, the choice being between a large field where home runs are hard to hit, or a small one where they come more easily. But whatever the dimensions a ball hit clean over the boundary is a home run. These dimensions also vary upwards. Some ball parks have a higher fence or wall than others on the boundary line, and in some the height varies along the line. On average foul lines run about three hundred and thirty feet to the boundary.

8

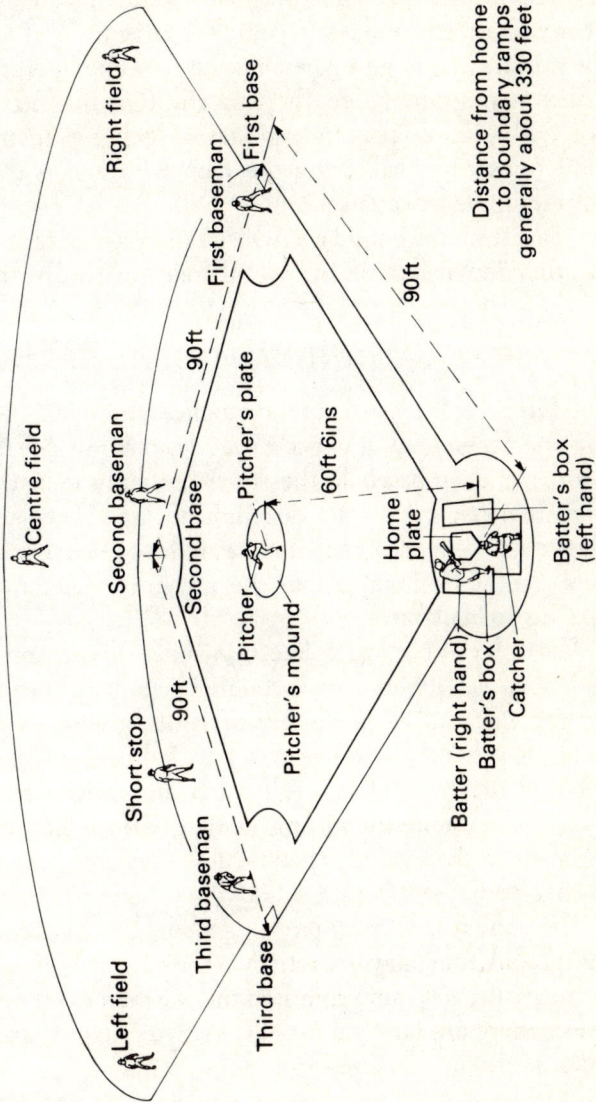

Right field

First base

First baseman

Distance from home to boundary ramps generally about 330 feet

Centre field

Second baseman

90ft

Second base

90ft

Pitcher's plate

Pitcher

60ft 6ins

Pitcher's mound

Home plate

90ft

Batter's box (left hand)

Short stop

90ft

Third baseman

Batter (right hand)
Batter's box
Catcher

Left field

Third base

The 'V' shaped foul lines determine the area of play and, in general, a ball hit over them is out of play. But there are exceptions to this. A fielder may be beyond the foul line when he makes a catch, and it still counts as an out. Or, if a ball hits the ground before going beyond the foul line, it is still a hit. Either it must be fielded beyond the foul line, or when it bounces back into play. If a spectator catches it, then various local rules apply, allowing the man who makes the hit to advance one or two bases.

Apart from the boundary, which can vary in size and shape, all other dimensions of the baseball field are fixed by the rules.

THE HITTING SIDE

The hitting side consists of nine men, eight fielders plus one, the one depending on which League is playing, for there are two Leagues in baseball, the American and the National. In the American the pitcher does not hit, and is replaced by a player called the designated hitter (who conversely does not field). In the National League the pitcher of the moment does take his turn at bat.

The order of batting is determined before the game begins and must be adhered to throughout. Substitutions in the batting side can be made, but are unforgiving. In baseball unlike in other American sports, once substituted for a player is out of the game. The result is that not much substitution takes place among the hitting/fielding side, at least not until the end of a close game, when tactics may determine whether to change players.

The same rule goes for pitchers, namely that once taken off the mound, they may not return in the same game. And while in the past it was more common for one man to pitch a whole game, there are now almost always two pitchers, and sometimes more, in every game.

THE PITCHER AND THE STRIKE ZONE

The pitcher is allowed to throw overarm and with a bent arm, to hurl the ball as hard as he can, although there are very specific rules about his action in preparing to throw. And one foot must not leave the rubber, the pitcher's plate, until after he has made the delivery.

If the pitcher throws the ball over home plate and at a height between the knees and armpits of the man at bat, and if the man at bat then misses the ball, it is called a strike.

The area thus defined is called the 'Strike Zone', and it looks like this from the pitcher's perspective:

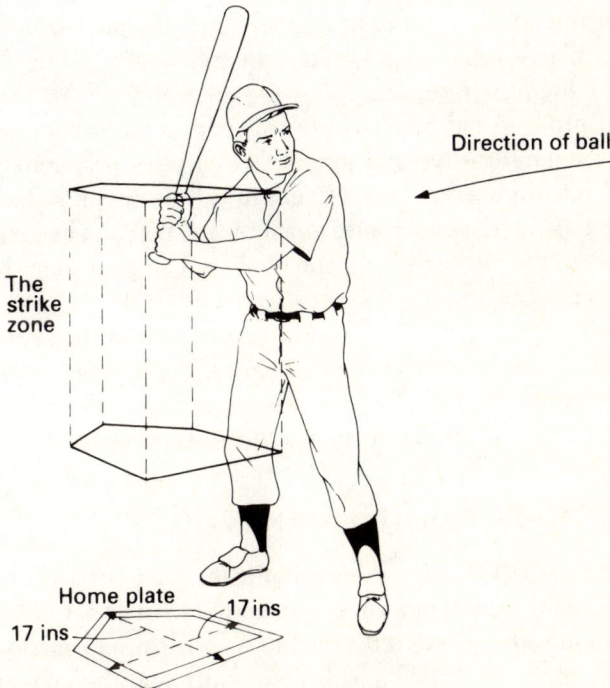

Direction of ball

The strike zone

Home plate   17 ins

17 ins

The strike zone is the area exactly over the home plate and between the shoulders and knees of the man at bat

The width of the strike zone is constant (the width of the plate), but its height is determined by the size of the man at bat.

Officially the distance between the front of home plate and the front of the pitcher's plate is the sixty feet and six inches mentioned before. But given that the pitcher's arm is in front of the rubber and that the batter's bat is also in front of home plate at the mid point of his swing, the actual distance the ball travels is nearer to fifty six feet.

The pitcher chosen must be notified to the umpires before the game. He must pitch until at least one man is either out or has moved to first base. Once the manager tells him to stop pitching, he cannot pitch again in that game. Generally the pitcher will be replaced between two and five times per side per game, or even more in a close game. If a pitcher is doing particularly well, he may pitch the whole game, but this is becoming less common.

In professional baseball the ball is pitched at somewhere between eighty-five and ninety-five m.p.h., occasionally at over one hundred m.p.h. Ninety m.p.h. is one hundred and thirty-two feet per second, which means that the ball travels between the pitcher's hand and the batter's bat in about half a second.

And that is why the veteran player Pete Rose says that hitting a baseball is the most difficult thing in sport. In doing so he quotes Ted Williams who is, with Rose, one of the half dozen greatest hitters of the last fifty years.

HOW A MAN IS OUT

Three strikes – three missed pitches that are accurately thrown into the strike zone – mean the man at bat is out.

On the other hand, if the pitcher throws the ball outside the strike zone, it is called a ball. Four 'balls' and the man at bat automatically walks to first base.

The man at bat can also be out if the ball is caught.

Whenever the man at bat hits the ball into fair territory, he must start to run to first base (or further if he chooses). If the ball is held by a fielder at the base to which the batter is running and the fielder's foot is on the base before the runner gets there, then the runner is out. Running between the bases he may also be tagged by a fielder holding the ball.

SCORING

To score: a runner must go round all four bases, running either when he hits, or when other batters behind him in the order hit; or he can hit the ball over the boundary line of wall or fence – a home run – in which case he and all runners on base score. This is a 'home run' and its value will depend on how many runners are on base.

THE BATTING ORDER AND THE INNINGS

The batting order may not be altered except for substitution.

When three men are out, the side is out – or 'retired' – and the other side goes in to bat. When three of their men are out, the inning is over and the first side bats again.

If the last man out in inning one was number four, then the next man to bat in inning two is number five, and so on.

(The numbers on players' shirts have nothing to do with their order in the batting. These numbers they keep for their career with the team. Retired players who have done long service with a team will keep their numbers as an honour.)

The game is won after nine innings unless:

(1) it is a tie, in which case the game goes on for complete innings until one or the other side wins.
(2) bad weather stops play in which case, if the game has gone five innings, the general rule is that the leader at this time takes the game.

13

THE LEAGUES AND THE SEASON

The World Series, as seen on Channel Four Television in October 1986, is the climax of a season that runs continuously from April until mid-October.

The teams competing in the World Series are the winners of the American and National Leagues.

There are fourteen teams in the American League and twelve in the National. Below this are the minor professional leagues, but there is no equivalent to promotion as in British soccer, and the only time a league franchise becomes vacant is when a team goes bankrupt. However some of the top minor league teams are what are called the 'farm' teams of the majors teams who own them and from which they promote players – or to which they demote them. Occasionally a franchise will move its location, as when the Brooklyn Dodgers went to Los Angeles. There is a Canadian team in each League: the Montreal Expos in the National, the Toronto Blue Jays in the American.

Each team plays about one hundred and sixty games a year, which means playing almost every day or evening, sometimes twice a day, in the five and half month long season until the world series. The teams in one League never play teams in the other except for occasional exhibition games and, informally, in pre-season training, known as 'spring training'. Some players do meet in the All Star game between the Leagues which takes place in early July each year. Players either being traded under their contract or changing teams as free agents often change League when they change team.

The Leagues are divided into eastern and western divisions, and the teams from each division play each other. But for scoring purposes they are kept separate and the leading team in one division plays the leading team in the other in a best of seven play-offs, the winners advancing to the World Series. It is a slightly arbitrary situation because eastern teams tend on average to be stronger than western and the second team in the eastern division may have more wins to its credit than the first team in the western. But, arbitrary as it may be, that is the way the game goes and Americans, for all their desire to invent new things, are also a very conservative people.

SUMMARY

- eight fielders, one pitcher.
- nine in the batting order, including the pitcher in the National League, a designated hitter (who does not field) in the American League.
- batting goes in fixed order (except for substitutions).
- three men out retires the side, and means the end of half an inning.
- nine innings make a game.
- men are out if struck out (three pitches missed in strike zone, or one of the first two balls in the strike zone hit foul which count as strikes) or if caught, or if run out.
- four balls out of the strike zone allow a batter to walk to first base and a runner on first to advance (and so on if there are runners all round the bases).
- the hitter scores by running to all four bases without being thrown out at a base or tagged between bases.
- or by hitting a home run over the boundary line.
- runners 'stranded' on bases at the end of an inning score nothing.
- there must be a result. There are no ties in baseball.

◇ 3 ◇

FIRST NOTES IN AN AMERICAN SYMPHONY

> My father grew up in Cleveland, and the Indians were his team. 'We had Nap Lajoie at second', he said, '. . . A great big broad shouldered fellow, but a beautiful fielder. He was a rough customer. If he didn't like an umpire's call, he'd give him a faceful of tobacco juice.'
>
> Roger Angell in *The Interior Stadium*

You cannot separate the rules of baseball from the way it is played and the way that play has evolved. No more can you separate the players from the crowd, which is not like the crowd in any other sport. Baseball crowds are raucous, but also knowledgeable. Baseball crowds hunger for the psychological satisfaction of victory or defeat, yet they are seldom violent. They watch a game into which no women have yet penetrated, yet there are a lot of women among the spectators. They drink a lot of beer, but they tend not to get drunk. Most baseball games start at 7.35 in the evening, and every week-day except Friday the next morning means that there is work or school to be gone to. They have a rhythm which fits the summer season and there are traditions that go with that rhythm, for example the crowd standing in turn around the stadium to make the 'wave' of humanity when they get bored, the 'seventh inning stretch', a tradition of

16

everyone standing up at the end of the seventh inning, the chanting of certain names and slogans.

Baseball is not expensive and twenty-five dollars or a little more will give you good seats for two, beer and soft drinks and hot dogs, a game programme, and public transport or parking. Twenty-five dollars is sixteen pounds sterling, but given the size of American wages in proportion to British take home pay, it represents a much lower sum. Most fans can afford to go to baseball games quite often and season tickets make the cost cheaper still. If you see a dull game, that is not the end of the world. You can go home early and hope for better next time. There are always a lot of children at baseball games, for if some adult does get violent or drunk, he gets ejected fast, usually to the crowd's pleasure. Out of town fans tend to be the more abusive, sometimes having come on a binge. But I have never felt scared at a baseball game, as I have at soccer games, even when taking young children.

The amount of glitter surrounding the game varies according to the team and the ball-park. At the older ones, like Fenway Park in Boston, there tend to be less mascots, dancing girls and score boards used not only for scoring but to entice the crowd with video-displayed slogans and piped fanfares.

Generally the sides out west tend to be more flamboyant than those in the east, but not always. There is, for example, a distinct difference between the older New York Yankees and the upstart New York Mets, the Yankees pin-stripes reminiscent of baseball uniforms in 1910, the Mets outfits much more garish and brightly coloured.

Knowing that baseball is intrinsically slow those who organize it are always anxious to introduce crowd pleasers, but in the end it does not seem to make much difference in attracting fans. Americans go to baseball matches to watch the game, and the game is in their blood. This is so much so that I cannot remember an American ever trying to explain baseball to me, as they might try to explain politics. They just seem to assume either that you know the game, or that you

17

come from another planet and there is little to be gained in trying to explain it.

But rest assured. Once the basis of the rules is grasped, baseball is not complicated. Once you get through the worst part, getting that basic understanding, all else follows easily. You just have to watch and absorb.

Remember one thing, however. Baseball is as much about the pitcher as the hitter. When television producers show excerpts, they tend to include those sections of the game in which runs are scored. True, a side needs to score to win, but it also needs to prevent the other side scoring, and great pitching can be just as interesting to watch as great hitting. In fact this is a game whose overall rhythm and character is determined by the fact that when the pitcher is on top, it is very difficult to hit the ball, let alone score. So if you forget about the pitcher, you forget about more than half the game.

Before the game begins the pitcher is allowed to warm up by throwing to the catcher. When he has done this, the umpire behind home plate calls play and the man at bat, number one in the order, steps into the batter's box, practices his swing and then takes his stance, bat held somewhat upright. The pitcher then takes his grip (which will determine how the ball will move or break in the air), hiding it from the man at bat in his gloved hand. He then swings his weight backwards, and assuming he is right handed plants his right foot on the rubber, winds up to pitch and throws. He may throw straight and fast, or he may make the ball swerve or 'break' in the air, a subject which is discussed more fully in the chapter on pitching (see p. 83 and what follows). For the moment appreciate that a pitch is not just being hurled with brute force. The success of good pitching against good hitters depends on deception, varying the pace of the ball from pitch to pitch, breaking it in different ways, upsetting the batter's prediction of the kind of pitch he thinks he is going to receive. And if you have watched baseball on television, there is a confusing point of definition here. A 'fast ball' is a straight

18

delivery that comes very fast, but a 'slow curve' is only relatively slow. It is still probably travelling between seventy and eighty miles an hour.

As the pitcher gets ready to throw, his body comes forward with the pitching arm and his left foot comes forward of the rubber, but the right foot may not leave it until the ball has left his hand. And he must go ahead with the pitch once he has wound up. He cannot step back and start again.

The pitch which we are watching at Fenway Park in Boston is straight, in other words over the plate and between knees and armpits of the man at bat. It is in the 'strike zone'. The hitter swings at it and misses, the catcher catches it clean and returns it to the pitcher.

The umpire now signals 'strike' and this is then shown on the scoreboard. There are a number of different score boards in different ball-parks around the country and all the major league grounds have ones that are digitally controlled, that can light up with a player's average and peformance as well as scores, batting orders, numbers of strikes and balls, etcetera. The ones I like are the old-fashioned ones, such as the one here at Fenway Park; with two sets of red lights, one for strikes, the other for hitters out; and one set of green lights, which show balls, that is balls thrown wide of the plate or too high or too low. I like it because it can't be missed yet is not obtrusive. You can keep it in the corner of your eye while chatting in a dull moment.

So far there is one red light, indicating one 'strike'.

The pitcher winds up and throws again. Again the man at bat swings and misses. Two red lights on the board: two strikes. The pitcher winds up once more, but this time the man at bat lets the ball pass. He judged it correctly as wide of the plate, and the umpire signals 'ball'. Two red lights and one green: two strikes and one ball. Another pitch and again the man at bat lets it pass, but the umpire declares strike by throwing his right arm outwards. The 'call' as it is known is unpopular with the man at bat, who turns to him and curses, but has to accept his fate. In Japan they argue with the umpire even more than in the major leagues in America, and apparently force him to change his mind quite often, bowing after the dispute is over. But this is America, not Japan. There is a kind of rather abstract respect among players for the better umpires, though not much courtesy shown in the heat of battle. American umpires do not change their minds. However it is generally acknowledged by American students of the game that most umpires judge the strike zone as being smaller than that officially laid down in the rules, the top of the zone being nearer to the belly button than the armpits.

Meanwhile, back to the game. The third red light has gone on the board, making three strikes and one ball, and the man out goes back to the dugout behind first base where his team mates sit. Then these three red lights go out and are replaced by another red light in a different row in the board. The side has one out.

The next man to bat has been standing in a small box just to the side of home plate, practicing swings. 'On deck' is the term for the man waiting to come to the plate and when he has practiced one or two more swings, he comes into the box, practices again and then gets ready for the first pitch. This comes and he lets it go, knowing it is a difficult pitch and having the wisdom or experience to do so because it is his first.

One strike. He swings at the next ball and misses. Two strikes. Then the next ball is wide, a 'ball', and so is the next and so is the next.

So the board now has on it:

One red light for the one out.
Two red lights for the two strikes.
Three green lights for the three balls.

Something now has to happen. If there is another ball, then the man walks to first base, that is gets a free walk. If the next pitch is called a strike by the umpire, then the side will be out. In fact the pitch it straight and he slugs it down the third base line, that is to the left of the field. It looks as if it might be a home run, but it is curving away too far to the left and falls into foul territory.

No lights show up on the board. However, had this happened before he had two strikes against him, it would have counted as a strike. But the rule says that so long as he is on the third strike, he can hit the ball into foul territory as often as he wants. So once again the pitcher winds up and throws. The ball is straight – or rather it is curving but heading for the strike zone over the plate – and the man at bat hits it, over the pitcher's head and just out of the reach of the short stop, so that it falls into the middle ground between the infield, in this case the short stop, and the man in left field, who has to run in to reach it.

The moment he hits the ball, the man at bat sprints off, dropping his bat as he does so. He 'makes' – get his foot onto – first base just ahead of the throw from the man in left field to the first baseman, who catches the ball and sends it back to the pitcher. (Running for a base it need not be the runner's foot that touches the plate. Runners in a hurry will slide, feet forward, or throw themself as if diving off the edge of the pool. Any part of their body in contact with the base makes them safe.)

The lights for strikes and balls go out, and the red light for outs stays at one. The next man on deck comes to bat.

The first pitch to the third man in the order is a strike, so is the second. He hits the third and it goes high into centre field where it is caught. This man is now out. However the man who is at first base has the opportunity to try to make another base after the moment of the catch. He starts off but then thinks better of it because the man in centre field would get the ball to the man at second base – they are not far from each other – before he, the runner, reached it. So he stays at first base.

The next man comes to bat. The first two pitches are strikes, the second two, balls. There is some tension now, because one more strike and the side will be out for the inning. On the other hand a successful hit would put two runners on base. And in fact this happens, with the next delivery. It is hit deep into right field, low and to the right of the right fielder who hurls himself forward in an attempt to make the catch. He misses and then has to pick himself up while the man at bat reaches first and the man on first reaches second. For a moment both wait and watch where he is going to throw.

The fielder throws the ball to second base and the runner, having gone a few paces to third makes a fast retreat, faster than he thought he would have to. It is a close call as to whether he is out or not, but the umpire declares that he is not. So the side, having been only one strike away from retiring now has runners at first and second base and another man to be struck out.

The ball is returned to the pitcher, but at this point the catcher comes forward onto the mound to talk to him, essentially to instruct him, because a catcher plays a crucial part in advising the pitcher (through signals behind the hitter's back) where to throw. This being a difficult moment, the catcher may want the pitcher to change tactics from something pre-arranged, or he may just want to reassure him.

The fifth man in the order now comes up to the plate, fifth because two are out, and two on the bases. The first throw is again a strike, and so is the second. They are faster pitches and fool the man at bat who is late with his swing. For the third time in this half of the inning the pitcher needs only one more strike to retire the side.

In fact the next delivery is a ball. The next is over the plate and hit, but sliced, going into the crowd like a bullet. And, as we saw before, because there are two strikes against the man already, he can hit foul now without it being counted as a strike. Indeed he does the same thing with the next pitch. And still the two pairs of red lights are on, auspiciously, one pair for the two outs, one pair for the two strikes. Again the pitcher winds up, throws and the ball is hit, looping high into left field. For a moment the crowd thinks – or hopes – that it is going to go over the wall, the particularly high boundary fence that Boston has.

But home runs need a bullet-like trajectory. Balls hit looping up also loop down as they lack momentum, and this one falls a yard short of the boundary line where it is caught. This means that the third out has been made and so the runners cannot move forward; for with the third man out, the side is retired, and the runners are 'stranded'. No score in the first half of the first inning. But it was close.

The opposition now come into bat. The first man is struck out on the first three pitches. The next man is caught by the pitcher on the second delivery, a ball hit so hard it knocks the pitcher over, but he holds the ball above the ground. Two down. It looks clinical.

Then the pitcher throws a ball. Then another. Two green lights. The next pitch is over the plate, low. Strike one. The Boston crowd cheer, but they are not so certain of the pitcher now and the next delivery is a ball. The lights show:

Two reds, for the two outs.
One red for the strike.
Three greens for the ball.

The pitcher may have been thrown off by the fall, or else he is trying to pitch a particular kind of delivery, one where the records or experience tell him that this man at bat has a weakness. But he is not getting it right. Or not so far.

If the next pitch is a strike, then Boston will only be one strike away from retiring the side. But if it is a ball, then the man will walk. After him comes the batting side's big home run hitter and this pitcher has not performed well against this hitter before. If . . .

It is of these 'if's' that baseball is made.

$\diamond$ 4 $\diamond$

RHYTHM AND DRAMA

A Breath of Fresh Air for 10 cents. A delightful sail
down the bay.
Slogan on an advertisement for the St George
Baseball Ground on Statten Island, c 1910.

Baseball and cricket have in common that they attract intense,
even obsessive, statistical analysis. E. W. Swanton and others
could and can quote at a moment's notice when in a final test
at Lord's there had previously been a fourth wicket part-
nership of eighty-four in failing light against two left-arm
bowlers. In just the same way baseball commentators and
pundits will tell you how such and such a left-handed hitter
for the Padres has done against right-handed Pittsburgh
pitchers in home games early in the season, etcetera. Out of
their simple basic rules each game is capable of producing
strings and meshes of numbers than run through the minds of
the initiate as equations of endless possibilities, for disaster or
success or just keeping things even.

Both games also attract some prose writing that is much
more than mere sports' reportage, the opposite end of the
literary scale to the rigid and only partly-telling precision of

numbers. All kinds of able American writers delight in baseball, Roger Angel, John Updike, Bernard Malmud (author of 'The Natural'), just as John Arlott, Neville Cardus and Edmund Blunden have made cricket literature part of good writing. Fundamentally it seems to be the rhythm of these small ball and stick games that makes for this kind of lazy, poetic prose, a rhythm that gives time, during the games and over the waxing and waning of the season, to look around, to work out not just how the games are played, but also how they exist as part of their respective societies, to make one American writer even declare that culture *is* baseball.

Baseball is a slow game, in some ways slower than cricket, not in terms of hours per match – baseball takes about three and a half – but certainly in terms of the hits and runs that you can expect per hour. Yet by another view it is a very fast game. If you look at the pitcher, you will see that he is working all the time, and working against time. The odds against him keep changing, with each inning, each batter, even each pitch. No one has many chances in baseball, and that means there is an intensity to each note played.

The symphony of my theme is the season. It begins with spring training in Florida or somewhere warm in the south-west. Before winter is over, fans are already following their teams in the local papers. They assess trades and curse the management, but as they watch the reports they find that the management is not all wrong and there is new hope in new faces. The regular season begins and they start to take serious notice. Some players are unexpectedly strong, others fail to fulfil promise. Through individual victories and defeats, the ideas are noted down like a musician's score and the ideas become phrases and movements. There are ritual moments, the All Star Game early in July and the Labour Day Holiday at the beginning of September. These are the beginnings and ends of the movements, but generally the climax is not revealed until near to the end itself.

This does not mean, of course, that every team has a chance

of leading its division, but how close in standard the major league teams are never fails to surprise me. There is never much difference in wins and defeats between the top and the bottom of the table. So even if your team is not winning, there is always the realistic chance that it will do so, or at least that you will see it moving up a point or two in the order, of ending on a strong note.

The point about how closely the major league teams are matched is worth reiterating because it means that very seldom is a match a foregone conclusion. The best teams frequently have off days, and pitchers have a great deal to do with victory and defeat. Even the best pitchers do not pitch well all the time, and the intensity of the game is such that a single hit can make the difference between defeat and victory. The New York Mets won the 1986 World Series but they trailed in so many games that, had they lost even half of them they would have been nowhere near the title. This is not to say that they were not a great team, the greater perhaps for their ability to come from behind. But a team does not get behind in a game which is a foregone conclusion. Or, another example from the 1986 season: in mid-September Boston led the Eastern Division of the American League with eighty-six wins and fifty-seven losses, looking like the eventual winners they would be, but on their tail were New York and Toronto each with seventy-eight wins, Detroit with seventy-six, and then Cleveland with seventy-three, Milwaukee and Baltimore with sixty-eight each. In other words, every team but Boston was within ten wins of each other, and Boston was only eighteen wins ahead of the team with the least wins. And this was with five months of the season gone. Compare any of the leagues over the months and while you may find a team in front from the start, often places are being shifted all down the order as the weeks go by. The drama is added to by the fact that games are played in series of three and a typical result might be that – say – Boston beat New York 5 – 4 and 6 – 3 in the first two but then New York beat Boston 9 – 2 in the third.

Nothing is certain and that is the underlying dramatic fact
about the season. That is what gives it the rhythm.

What is true about the tension that exists throughout the
season is true about the series of games between teams – not
the World Series, but the regular series of three that take
place throughout the same period. What is true about the
tension in a series is true about the individual game. And
what is true about the game is true about the inning. Nothing
is certain until it is played out, and I do not know a major sport
where the teams are so closely matched. Within this dramatic
framework – the good guys, your side, and the bad guys, the
opposition very closely matched – is the true framework of
the individual game. Symphony to note, season to individual
play sub scenes and sub text, the tension between pitcher and
hitter – it does not matter what analogy you choose. If it is
true that the structure of music and drama are mirrors of the
structure of life, then the same is true of baseball. The more
you sense this, the more you enjoy baseball. And the more
you bring to the game, in terms of knowledge of players, of
their averages, overall and against other players and sides, of
tactics in the field, of the way pitchers perform or may be
expected to perform, the more you enjoy the game, the more
you become involved in that pleasure which is secondary
only to playing, namely talking or reading about it. Baseball
is one way in which you can communicate with almost any
American. The idea that baseball is culture is not without
veracity.

To return to the question of whence comes a game's
tension, I want to go back and look at the individual plays
recorded in the previous chapter, those few hits and misses
that made up an inning and a half of an imaginary game. It
started with one man struck out quite quickly.

The first pitch was a strike, so was the second. The next two
were balls, the next a strike. The man at bat was dismissed.

This is a small part of the drama – the smallest – but it is
drama all the same. After two pitches the batter either had to

score with the next pitch, or get a ball. Luckily he got a ball, but only a short reprieve. Once again he either had to score or get a ball. Luckily for him the pitch was again a ball, another reprieve. So whereas everything was loaded against the man at bat after the first two pitches, which were strikes, now things were beginning to turn against the pitcher. On the next pitch he either had to strike the man out or, if he threw a ball, he would be in a situation where, after one more ball the man would get an automatic walk to first base. In fact on the next pitch the man was struck out.

The elegance of baseball lies fundamentally in its detail, in the way that, with each pitch, the odds change a little. With each man at bat they do the same. With one man safely out, the pitcher seems secure, more so when he had two strikes against the next man, even more so when the second man was caught. But then the next man hit the ball over short stop's head and reached first base. The situation was still not too bad for the pitcher, but with a man on base the side at bat were looking at the game differently. They had more hope. A moment before, their lead off batters had been quickly out. Now they had a runner on first base. Or, you can begin to express it from the pitching side's point of view: two outs and *only* one runner on a base. Not too good for the hitting side.

But then it changed around again. The next man drove the ball into right field, putting himself on base and advancing the runner from first to second. This looked really good, but remember it was a last-minute event. The man who made the hit into right field already had two strikes against him. One more strike and the side would have been retired, the inning a non-event for the hitting side.

Once again the 'count', as it is called, went to none and two, no balls, two strikes. There were two men on the bases, but again the pitcher was within one strike of retiring the side. One more strike, and the pitcher would be safe. One more strike and the hits will add up to . . . nothing.

But instead of a strike the man hit the ball very hard – only

28

not hard enough. A home run would have put the team three ahead with only two outs in the first inning, a very serious situation for the pitcher and his side. Instead what might have been a home run became a relatively easy catch in the outfield, the batting side was retired and the pitcher could breathe easily again.

This imaginary game would have now been going for somewhere between eight and twelve minutes with the ebb and flow of the drama changing frequently. And remember that the contestants are anonymous. Think of the difference in a cricket match between knowing and not knowing the players. My description is therefore essentially clinical, baseball seen as you might see an operation by a surgeon on television, but knowing nothing of either the doctor's or the patient's background, and while the game is slow if measured by hits or runs, measured by the pitcher's fortunes it is much more like a soccer match, the ball and action switching from one end to the other and back again.

But here any analogy with soccer breaks down. Individuals are important in all team sports, but in baseball the struggle is very much concentrated round the particular pitcher and hitter, a struggle in which the pitcher has the advantage, at least as the game is defined by its rules and dimensions. Which brings me back to the point made earlier about the mistake made by those who watch only for the hits. Baseball is a game loaded against hitting the ball and Ted Williams, who retired in the early 'sixties, was the last major league hitter to average .400, the average being worked out by dividing the number of official times a player bats by the number of hits that land the hitter on a base. For example, if a player is 'up' three times in a game, and gets one hit, he has a .333 average. But this is very high, and for over thirty years no one in major league baseball has hit safely and reached first base four times in ten times at bat. Indeed today .350 is extraordinary and, while a few hitters may make .400 for a few games, they never keep it up.

The point is not only that a baseball is very hard to hit, but that in addition there is very little room for defensive play. The man at bat can hope for a ball or two, or he can let the first straight pitch go, even the second. But that minimal amount is all the freedom he has. And then, if he does hit the ball, he is doing so with a curved bat which means that if he hits a few millimetres off the bat's centre the ball may fly in the air to be caught. Even if he hits it low, he has to place it cleverly and then run like hell to cover the ninety feet to first base in time. Batters fielded cleanly by an infielder are almost always thrown out at first, and if the man at bat hits the ball too far to make an easy pick up for an outfielder he may also be out at the base. It is a very hard game in which to score, and, while critics rate this boring, those who love the game believe it engenders character and intensity. Indeed baseball has even been called a 'non-game' by some American writers, not in a sense of putting it down, but rather as a way of defining it as a game in which everything is loaded against scoring.

The score in a typical game will look like this:

First Inning	0–0
Second	0–0
Third	1–0
Fourth	2–0
Fifth	0–0
Sixth	0–0
Seventh	1–3
Eighth	0–1
Ninth	0–1

That is the bare score but from this it is possible to see that neither side is ever safe. The largest the margin gets up to the sixth is three ahead but, while pleasant for the side that holds lead, this is not a comfortable margin. (Indeed no moment in major league baseball is comfortable until the game is over. At Fenway Park I have seen thousands of fans mooch out of the park at the end of the seventh when Boston was four ahead, only for the side to be overtaken in the eighth or ninth.)

Now I will add to those same figures the numbers of runs, with in brackets beyond them the number of runners stranded on a base:

First Inning	0(0)–0(2)
Second	0(0)–0(3)
Third	1(1)–0(1)
Fourth	2(0)–0(0)
Fifth	0(0)–0(3)
Sixth	0(1)–0(0)
Seventh	1(0)–3(2)
Eighth	0(2)–1(1)
Ninth	0(3)–1(1)

You now see that the side that was leading until the last inning was the side which scored runs, but the side that was making more hits was loosing all the way, with six men stranded on bases in the first three innings, runners who, had they reached home, would have made for a significant lead.

Or, look at the end of the game: the side which was being caught up left five men on bases in the last two innings. Indeed in the last inning they had the bases 'loaded', a runner on every one, but could not quite pull it off.

The idea is not to fill the reader's head with figures, but to show that in almost each half of each inning the possibilities were wide open, and changing all the time, and that the runs scored in the game reveal only a small part of the action.

'If only X had not been caught, or Y had not been struck out, or Z had not made a fielding error . . .'. That is what baseball is about. If only.

◇ 5 ◇

SYMMETRIES AND SIZES

'It is the symmetry that is so perfect. Five feet, even
two feet more or less between the bases and baseball
would be quite different.'
        Ben Mondor, President of the Minor League
                                Pawtucket Red Sox.

The baseball as used in professional games consists of:

– a spherical piece of cork
– a black layer of rubber over the cork
– a red layer of rubber over the black layer
– one hundred and twenty-one yards of blue grey wool. (By
  now the total weight is two and seven-eighth ounces).

Then:

– forty-five yards of white wool
– on top of the white wool: fifty-three yads of blue grey wool,
  followed by
– one hundred and fifty yards of fine cotton.

These are all wound taut by machine; when the process is
complete, a coat of rubber cement is put over the whole, with a
similar coat on the two pieces of cowhide that make up the
outer covering.

33

Each of the pieces of cowhide is in the shape of a figure of eight, or rather an eight where the circles do not meet in the centre, held together on the finished ball by two hundred and sixteen stitches of red thread, sewn by hand. This done, the cowhide is made slightly damp and the ball put into a machine to flatten out the stitches.

The final weight must be not less than five ounces and not more than five and a quarter. The circumference of the ball must be more than nine and less than nine and a quarter inches.

If this sounds a little obsessive with detail, it is. Americans can be obsessional about detail and one way they take it out on each other is through baseball. For all that, games succeed or fail by being played within the rules and most of the rules reflect the established physical dimensions. A differently made baseball would either be too lively or too dead, would either break in the air too much or not at all. It is these things which Americans rave about when they talk about symmetry in baseball. (The Official Baseball Rules, published by the American *Sporting News* can, by the way, be obtained in England; Appendix III suggests where to get them.)

Rules about bats are not so obsessive as those about the ball, or rather not so exact. Rule 1.10 (a) states that: 'The bat shall be a smooth, rounded stick not more than two and three quarter inches in diameter at the thickest part and not more than forty-two inches in length. The bat shall be: (1) one solid piece of wood, or (2) formed from a block of wood consisting of two or more pieces of wood bonded together with an adhesive in such a way that the grain direction of all pieces is essentially parallel to the length of the bat . . .

Beyond this the exact standards of lamination are complicated but the rule essentially is saying that any laminated bat must be as strong as a one piece bat – broken bats are not uncommon and a flying piece of bat dangerous to home plate umpires and catchers. Nor must they have a greater hitting power than solid bats. In addition makers must be approved, before being allowed to sell bats in the professional leagues, by the Rules Committee which is established by an over-seeing group representing professional and amateur players from the American and National League, and the National Association which also governs amateur baseball.

The bat handle may be treated with a foreign substance to improve grip, but only down to eighteen inches. As regards the thickness of the bat, the two and three-quarter inch rule about diameter translates to approximately eight and three-quarter inches in circumference. And while most bats take advantage of the maximum dimension allowed, many are a lot shorter than the forty-two inches allowed, today generally being between thirty-five and thirty-seven inches long. Bats used to be longer but today are not only shorter but also lighter, weight also being lost by making the handles slim. A small cup shaped indentation at the bottom of the bat is allowed and this is used as a way of affecting the thickness to weight ratio, in other words to assist the bat designer to create the lightest bat of the maximum allowed thickness. Bats are made of Northern White Ash, a tree which mainly grows in the mountains of New York and Pennsylvania, trees suitable for bat-making being cut after about forty years. They used to be made of hickory which is harder, but less springy than Northern White Ash. There are hundreds of variations in the way bats are made and balanced. Between them two leading makers, Adirondack and Hilerich & Bradbury make over three hundred and fifty different models. Each costs over eight dollars (or about eight pounds sterling) and breaks are frequent, especially against fast pitchers.

Well made wooden bats, as opposed to cheaper models or aluminium bats (not allowed in professional baseball) taper towards the end and the point of the bulge is called the 'sweet spot', whence the swinging wood will give maximum impact to the ball.

The next specific is the glove. Rules 1.12–1.15 specify its

dimension and construction in prose that might be written by a solicitor. For example:

Rule 1.13. 'The first baseman may wear a leather glove or mitt not more than twelve inches long from top to bottom and not more than eight inches wide across the palm, measured from the base of the thumb crotch to the outer edge of the mitt. The space between the thumb section and the finger section of the mitt shall not exceed four inches at the top of the mitt and three and one half inches at the base of the thumb crotch . . .' And so on . . . And this is only for the first baseman.

Simplified, there are three different kinds of padded leather mitt allowed by the rules. The catcher is allowed the largest, thirty-eight inches in circumference, in other words about sixteen or seventeen inches wide depending on the thickness. The first baseman is also allowed a large glove and it is reckoned that its length can add eighteen inches to his height when reaching for a ball above his head. The gloves worn by the pitcher and the rest of the fielders are also defined by the rules under one heading, although in practice they vary considerably. The pitcher's glove has solid webbing (as opposed to a lattice) between the fingers and thumb so as to hide the ball. Infielders' gloves tend to be stubbier than outfielders', and the latter have been described as 'butterfly nets'. Another rule states that the pitcher's glove must be uniform in colour and must not be white or grey. Traps would be a better name than gloves for these pieces of equipment.

Rules also define uniforms, helmets and shoes, but these do not particularly affect the actual play of the game. The rules also state that a dug-out must be provided for each hitting side, and a bull-pen where pitchers sit, and may practice when they are likely to be called in to the game. The bull-pen is connected to the coach in the dug-out by telephone, always an internal line, for when an outside line was tried pitchers became incommunicado, talking to their wives or girl friends at the club's expense.

The home plate is made of heavy vinyl, four inches thick, and has a weight of about twenty pounds. It has five sides, forming a rectangle with a triangle on the top, the apex of the triangle pointing away from the pitcher's mound. The plate is seventeen inches wide and twenty-three inches long at the longest point, off-white, except for the sloping edges which are black, making them easier for the pitcher to see.

Home plate is just stuck into the ground with spikes. The other bases, or 'bags' – as opposed to home *plate* – are square, fifteen inches wide and long and three inches thick. They are made of softer and lighter material and anchored to a projectile coming up through the ground from a solid concrete block dug into the ground. The pitcher's plate, the 'rubber', is twenty-four inches long, four sided, and six inches wide.

The pitcher's mound (see diagram on p. 38) has a nine foot radius and the centre of it is fifty-nine feet from the back of home plate, but the rubber is set another eighteen inches behind the centre of the mound, making sixty feet and six inches the theoretical distance between pitcher and hitter.

Six inches in front of the rubber the slope begins, running downwards at the ratio of one inch to one foot for the next six feet. More simply, the base of rubber is raised six inches above the rest of the field.

The batter's box, in which he must stand, is opposite home plate. It stands (see diagram on p. 39) six inches away from the side of the plate, is six feet long (taking length as the axis on which the ball travels from pitcher to hitter) and is four feet wide. There are two batters' boxes, one for right-handers, one for left-handers.

Behind the batter's boxes is the catcher's box, which is about six feet long and a little less than four feet wide (see diagram on p. 39). There are also boxes provided for the next man at bat, and the first and third base coaches. These are the only coaches allowed near the field, and they assist players by signals on when to run, particularly when a runner is moving in the opposite direction from the ball. For example, if the ball

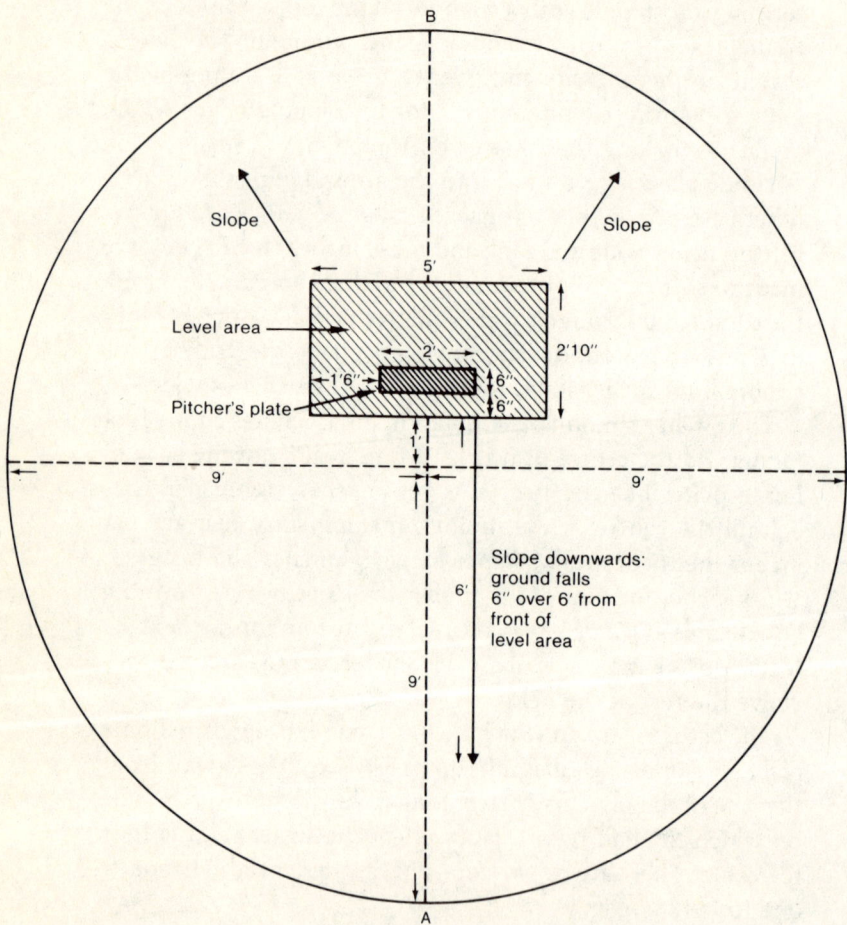

B

Slope   Slope

5'

Level area

2'

Pitcher's plate

1'6"   2'10"

6"
6"

9'   9'

1'

Slope downwards:
ground falls
6" over 6' from
front of
level area

6'

9'

A

Level area on
pitcher's mound

A   B

| Uniform slope from here to here | | Gradual slope to back of
mound |

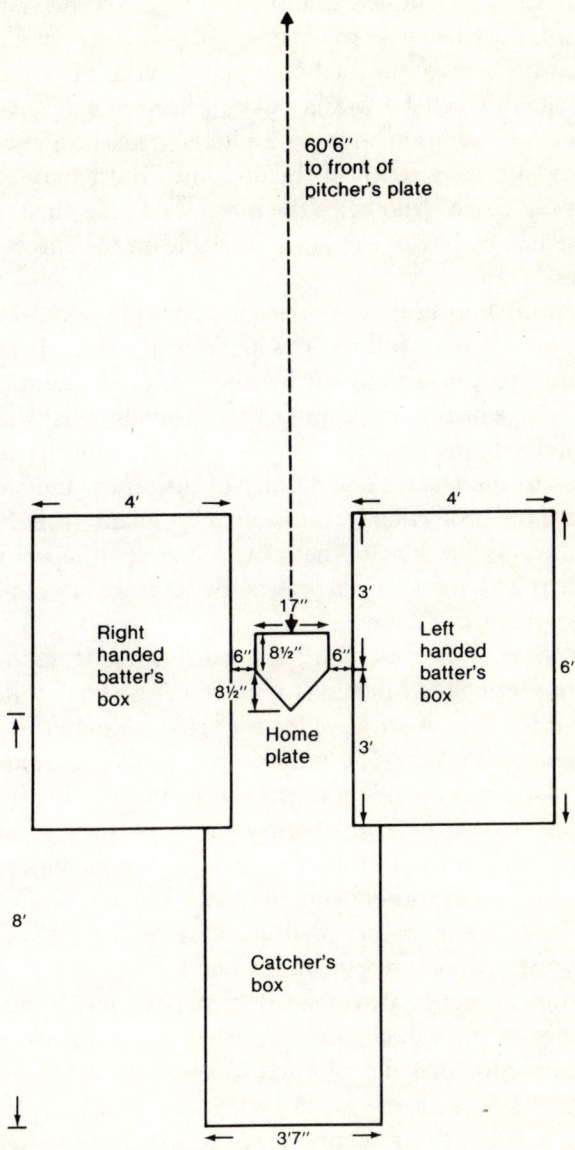

60'6"
to front of
pitcher's plate

4'

17"

8½"

Right
handed
batter's
box

6"

6"

3'

Left
handed
batter's
box

8½"

Home
plate

3'

6'

Catcher's
box

8'

3'7"

is hit hard into right field and the runner at second starts off for third, the third base coach may judge that he should stop at third or keep going for home plate. Were the runner to judge this himself he would have to keep looking over his shoulder. In addition there is a pitching coach in the bull-pen, and a hitting coach in the dug-out. There may also be a 'dug-out coach' who helps the manager decide on strategy, particularly by having statistics available on the opposition's players.

There are four umpires in the game, one at each base; they are discussed more fully in chapter eleven. There is also an official scorer provided by the League President. He sits in the press box, which is something that grounds must provide, high above home plate. He carries a lot of authority and 'is entitled to the respect and dignity of his office, and shall be accorded full protection by the League President' (rule 10.02). The rule goes on to state that 'The scorer shall report to the President any indignity expressed by any manager, player, club employee . . .' etc.

A distinction is important here. The umpire is responsible for interpreting the rules and his decisions are final. If he calls a ball, it is a ball. A strike called is a strike. A man run out at first base is run out. The umpire has absolute authority in these matters and it is up to the scorer to record them. For example, if a man bats out of order, the scorer must record the fact, but not inform the umpire; it is up to him to notice at the right time. On the other hand, the scorer can tell the umpire if he calls the inning before three men are out.

The distinction in responsibility between the official scorer and umpire is not easy to make, or rather can only be made by reference to individual rules. In broad terms the umpire is responsible for making calls according to the rules, and the scorer for assessing values. In particular a number of factors can be charged to or against players that do not affect the score, but do affect the statistics of the player and the team – fielders' 'errors' and 'assists', for example, runs batted in, sacrifices and earned runs (all of which are defined in chapter seven).

Americans as a nation have always loved numbers, computers, statistics, and results – and baseball gives results. In other words, baseball begins with numbers, (the dimensions) and ends with numbers (the batting, fielding, pitching, team and individual statistics, the placing in the league, the reckoning of away and home wins and losses, the rate of improvement or decline of a side). Between these numbers comes the play itself, the strategy and the finer points of interpretation of the basic rules.

◇ 6 ◇

VARIATIONS ON
THE THEME

> The Red Sox have a runner at third base, and one out.
> The batter hits a long fly ball to right centre against
> the Yankee pitcher. The ball deflects off the right
> fielder's glove and floats into the centre fielder's
> mitt. . . . Is the batter out? and . . . can the runner
> tag up after the ball touches the centre fielder's mitt?
> From *Baseball Brain Teasers* by Dom Forker

The object of baseball is to hit the ball and move to a base, then
hope that players behind you in the order hit it again and so
forth until you round all four bases and run home, thereby
scoring.

You can be out if you are caught. You can be struck out,
after three strikes have gone into the strike zone, that is over
the plate and between the knees and armpits of the man at bat.
(For a time one or two teams tried to have midget hitters,
thereby reducing the height of the strike zone to eighteen
inches, but the notion soon proved ludicrous.)

You can also be out by being tagged by a fielder holding the
ball before you reach the base, or by the baseman holding the
ball thrown to him and having his foot or part of his body on
the base before you get there.

Perhaps the elegance of all great games is that they start
from simple rules, and essentially this is it as far as Baseball's

42

elementary rules go. For example in soccer you could say that all you have to do is to kick the ball through the goal without fouling, letting the ball out of the game or being off side. The strategy is to win, simple; the tactics are endless. Here are some of them, seen from both the pitcher's and the hitter's point of view.

Intentional Walk, sometimes called a sacrifice walk: In certain situations, or against certain good hitters, particularly home run hitters, the pitcher may deliberately decide to let the player at bat walk to first base. Particularly if a team is hanging on to a one run lead or is tied at the end of a game, or if there are runners on second and/or third base at the time that a big home run hitter comes up to bat, the pitcher may just throw the ball wide to the catcher so that the hitter has no chance of hitting.

Hitters can, of course, hit a ball – a ball wide of the strike zone – if they want to, so long as they keep their feet in the batter's box, but generally they let it go, or have to let it go, because it is too wide. When a pitcher decides to create a sacrifice he will generally throw the ball well wide of the man at bat and to the opposite side on which he holds the bat, thereby making it almost impossible to hit.

Just occasionally, but very occasionally, a pitcher will fool a man at bat by throwing him a couple of deliberately wide pitches and then one over the plate, hoping that he will be caught off guard and hit a fly ball, that is hit it into the air so that it can be easily caught.

The Order of Batting: There are nine men in the batting order. (By the way, I use the word men not to be chauvinist but because, either for chauvinist, physical or social reasons there are no women in professional baseball.)

As we have seen, the nine men consist of:

In the National League, eight fielders and the pitcher of the moment.

In the American league, eight fielders and a designated hitter, a hitter who never fields.

Rather like a batting order in cricket, the tendency is to work down from strength at the top of the order to weakness at the bottom. But there are variations on this.

Hitters, the good ones, *tend* to be divided into steady midfield hitters and home run sluggers. The former *tend* to have the highest averages in the league, above .350 hits per time at bat if they are very good. Home run sluggers often do not have very high averages, but home runs are also shown on a performance sheet. Over thirty home runs a year is excellent. Sixty one is the all time record, held by Roger Maris of the New York Yankees.

The point of the distinction is that the tendency in developing an order is to put a couple of steady hitters to lead off, with the big sluggers in the middle of the order. This means that if the lead-off hitters are one and two, you hope they will get to first and second base and then follow with a home run. A home run can count anything from one – if there is no one on base – to four for a 'grand slam', when the bases are 'loaded', in other words when there are runners at first, second and third before the home run is hit.

In a sense, however, this ordering lacks logic because if the last man out in one inning was number seven, you lead off with eight and nine and then follow them with number one. If the last man out in the previous inning was number two and your first man in the next is number three, he may be a home run hitter and so the idea of the order is gone. But the logic does come into play at the end of the game, for mathematically those at the top of the order are likely to bat more times than those at the bottom.

Hitting tactics are also determined by the choice of right- and left-handers. A left-handed hitter will generally find a right-handed pitcher easier to deal with, and vice versa. Because of this some hitters such as Pete Rose develop the technique of 'switch' hitting. In other words they can bat right- and left-handed with just about equal ability. They will go left-handed against right-handers and vice versa. But they are rare, so managers tend to pick a balance of right- and left-handers, and some coaches will load their sides in particular ways on particular days, depending on who is pitching.

Because the human population tends to be right-handed, left-handers tend to be more highly valued, particularly if they are pitchers.

The Ordering of Pitchers: This is a simple rule – a lead-off pitcher is chosen for the day by the coach, and generally announced beforehand. He can pitch for as long or short a time as the coach wants him to, so long as he has finished pitching to one man, who must either be out or have reached at least first base. Once taken out of the game, the pitcher is out of it for good. So while a game may feature five or six pitchers, the general rule is two or three. It is greatly to a pitcher's credit if he pitches the whole game. When a team is behind later in the game the pitcher will generally be changed and sometimes if the coach feels that a pitcher's strength is waning, or his luck running out, he will be changed if the team is ahead.

Generally it takes about five days for a pitcher's arm to repair itself after a pitching stint in a game, which means that a team's best pitcher can only be used about once every five days. As a team is most unlikely to have more than that number of top-class starting pitchers, developing a 'rotation' is a key part of the manager's strategic skills. Managers need victories, but not easy victories, nice as they may be, and a top pitcher may be wasted against a weak team with a weak pitcher.

If you have watched the World Series on Channel Four, you will see the manager in tense moments struggling with a list. This is a digest of statistical information that tells him what pitcher is strong against what hitter and vice-versa and his conclusion can be crucial for the success of a game. There is nothing more disheartening than to see a pitcher who has done well for about six innings taken out in favour of a relief pitcher, who is then hit around the field. On the other hand there is nothing more encouraging than to have a relief pitcher, brought in when a pitcher or pitchers are being hit around, take control of the other side.

The statistical information that exists for a manager's use is compendious. He will know which pitchers are stronger at home than away, which have a particularly good record in which ball-park, which do well against which hitters or types of hitters, which go consistently well for how many innings when starting a game, which play best in losing situations and so on. Because the margins in professional baseball are so narrow, because, that is, teams are so equally matched, it is considered by some American pundits that what separates the great managers from the rest is their ability to organize a rotation that gives them consistent victories. Indeed, if you ever hear anyone argue that the scouts pick the new talent, that the talent plays the game, that the specific pitching and hitting and base coaches do the training, that the statisticians collect the statistics and that the managers do little more in baseball than collect large cheques, look important and shout at the umpires, then you should suggest that managers also organise rotations.

Bunting: Generally the art of hitting a baseball involves hitting it hard, either really hard so that it goes over the wall for a home run, or hard enough to land it in the zone between the infield and the outfield. Placing the ball is the key to successful hitting, whether driving it through the gaps between the bases, or into the area between the infield and the outfield. Remember that generally there is little defensive play for a hitter, except to let pitches go by him as strikes. Better players such as Wade Boggs can hit defensively by hitting pitches they do like over the foul lines, but they are rare. There is however, bunting which, if not quite defensive play, is an alternative to hitting the ball with a full swing.

Bunting involves tapping the ball, and it is a very great art, because if tapped too hard it goes straight either to the pitcher or to first or third base, and the hitter will not have time to reach first base. Conversely if it is tapped very softly the catcher can run forward, pick it up and throw it to first base a lot faster than the hitter can run there.

It is, however, always great to see, because if done correctly it comes as a surprise to pitcher, fielders and spectators. And doing it correctly is not easy, partly for the reasons mentioned above, namely that the ball will go too far or too short a distance, and because the hitter finds it difficult to deceive and take a normal stance and appear to hit the ball hard before sliding his hand down the bat for a bunt. Ideally, only once the ball is in the air, or nearly in the air, should the man at bat move his hands down it so as to push rather than swing at the ball. But this is almost impossible given the speed of pitches.

Bunting comes and goes. One can see several games without it being tried as a tactic, for a player who does it well must never do it too often, or any potential element of surprise is lost. And often it does not succeed, so coaches, at least conservative ones, do not feel comfortable with it. Indeed many coaches are themselves out of their depth with it, unable to teach the art. To counter this one or two coaches run special clinics to teach bunting at spring training in the south, before the regular season.

Bunting can be used – indeed is best used – as a form of sacrifice. If there is already a runner on base, the person who bunts may not get to first base in time, but may enable the person who is on first to get to second, or second to get to third, etcetera. And that will be worthwhile if it is judged that a base advance is worth the out.

In general bunting is seen more in the National than the American League, the reason being that pitchers (who have to hit in the National League) are often very weak hitters. At least making contact with the ball is easier when bunting than when swinging at it.

Sacrifice Fly: It is easier to hit a baseball high and into the middle distance than it is to hit it low and into the infield, or right the way over the boundary line for a home run. There are a number of reasons for this. One is that the ball must travel downwards from the pitcher's arm, in his raised position on the mound, in order to be in the strike zone. The ball is thus travelling through two planes, downwards and forwards, whereas the bat is only travelling through one, and as the ball comes downwards to the bat, the tendency is to hit it with the upper curved edge, thereby making it travel upwards.

Put slightly differently, it is easier to slice at a pitch than to hit it square on. The problem is that a slice is likely to go high and curving upwards, high enough to give a fielder time to move and make the catch. Essentially it is called a fly ball, this kind of hit, and is generally what pitchers try to get players to hit, and what hitters try to avoid doing.

But just as a sacrifice bunt can have benefits, so can hitting a fly ball when there are other men on base. In particular with a runner on third base, a fly ball hit into centre or right field means that he can start moving the moment the catch is made. Because it is unlikely that an outfielder in the centre or to the right can throw the ball to home plate in one, there may just be time to make the run before the ball reaches the catcher. If the run – or the advance of a base – is crucial, then the sacrifice is worth it.

Stealing a Base: Normally players do not advance between the bases unless the ball is hit, but a player who is on base may run the moment the pitcher makes his delivery. He can do this if a ball (or a strike) is pitched, but not if the ball is hit foul.

There is a runner on first and a man at bat. The moment the pitcher throws, the man on first begins to run. A number of possibilities then occur:

If it is a ball, and he can get to second base before the catcher throws it to the second baseman, then he is allowed to stay at second.

If it is hit as a ground ball, in other words if the hit ball touches the ground before being fielded, forcing the man at bat to run, the man running to second has a slight start. It is possible that the man at bat will be run out at first, but the man starting from first will get to second before the first baseman can throw the ball to the second baseman.

If it is a fly ball he must go back to base, so that he does not start running until after the ball has been caught. Then he can try his luck or stay where he is.

There is more to stealing bases than just that. A fast runner on first, a person with a reputation for steals, can do a lot to upset a pitcher. He will edge forward from the base just before the throw and force the pitcher to send the ball to first base as a way of holding him down. A regular tussle of cat and mouse can then ensue with the runner trying to throw the pitcher off balance and the pitcher in turn throwing off balance the man's attempts to steal. The most dramatic bluff comes when the pitcher, knowing the man is going to try to steal, allows him to get away with it, pitching a ball wide of the hitter which the catcher then throws to second base, a play which requires great speed and accuracy by the catcher and needs the second baseman to be in position right on the base, whereas he usually stands a little apart from it.

Some players have great stealing records and one, Ricky Henderson, once made 130 steals in a season, the all time record. A high number of steals can make a very significant difference to a team's overall performance. It is also possible to steal from second, or to make a double steal, with two runners stealing at the same time. Stealing from third is possible but rare, because the ball will go to the catcher and he can prevent the man running by simply holding on to the ball.

But it does happen, if the catcher drops the ball or throws it to second base to stop a steal from first.

But, unlike bunting, where a reputation does not help because the fielding side are ready for the player, a reputation for stealing can affect fielding tactics considerably. As already discussed it can put an experienced pitcher off his rhythm, allowing him no leeway in terms of walks, and it can also affect the fielding. Both first base and second have to stay right on the bases, thereby opening the gap into which a ground ball hit can be directed.

And a great steal is a thrill to watch. First there will be cat and mouse between the pitcher and the man on base. It will go on, with ball after ball being sent to the first or second baseman and the attempting runner having to move back and get onto the base. Then perhaps there will be a strike and the man on base will perhaps not try to move at all. Suddenly, just when you think he has given up trying to steal, he is off and at the base in the blink of an eye. It is attractive to watch.

Double Plays are even more exciting. This is when two men are out in the same play, involving considerable fielding ability. The ball has to be fielded, thrown to one base, and then to the other, in the time it takes a runner to get to a base. For example, if there is a runner on first base and the ball is hit to the short stop, the short stop throws it to second base forcing out the man who is now running from first to second, and the second baseman throws it to first base, forcing out the man who has made the hit. Alternatively, if a ball is caught in the outfield and after the catch a runner at third tries but fails to make home plate and is out, that also is a double play.

Double plays also have the dramatic effect of giving a side and spectators more than they hoped for. The pitcher may be in a hole with two men on bases and no outs. The pitch is then hit, threatening to put men on all three bases, to 'load' the bases. But instead of that, two are out and the threat from the batting side looks very different.

Triple plays are known, but rare.

ENLARGING
THE GLOSSARY OF
THE GAME

Baseball has a lot of language attached to it, names of things, names of places, names that have other meanings in other languages. Some of it is official, some unofficial. There is a great deal of slang attached to baseball, so that a 'laugher' is that rare thing, a game being won so easily the batting/fielding side can sit back and relax. Some words do not mean quite what they suggest, so that a 'junk man' is not a description of a useless player, but a phrase used to describe a pitcher who relies mainly on 'off speed' pitches and their variation, 'junk' or unorthodox pitches. Variation is, of course, the key to the art of pitching, and a player who is fooled by the speed of a pitch, expects a breaking ball and gets a fastball, is 'deked' with a hard 'e', slang for decoyed. On the other hand someone – hitter or pitcher – who can get through tough spots is know as a 'clutch'-hitter or 'clutch'-pitcher.

'Up the alley' means up the alley between two fielders; a

ball hit up the alley is called a 'tweener', usually leading to a double or triple or, rarity of rarities, an 'inside the park homer'.

'Down the alley' does not apply to hitting down the foul lines or even into midfield, but rather to the middle of the strike zone. A pitch 'down the alley' is a bulls-eye pitch and seldom to be tampered with. Even more so, 'in the hole' does not mean what it sounds like because again it applies to pitchers who are very much above ground. A pitcher is 'in the hole' when he is behind by two pitches, when the count is two balls and no strikes or three balls and one strike. 'The hook' is another term applied to pitchers. It is what the manager does when a pitcher is faring badly and the manager comes out to the mound. He gives him the hook. A 'hitch' on the other hand is a term applied to batters. A hitch is a flaw in a batter's swing and is what every boy must not have. For all that, some of the greats have been successful even with a hitch. 'Foot in the bucket' is another term to do with batting action which is again not quite as bad as it sounds. Someone who stands with a 'foot in the bucket' does not have his front foot pointing towards the pitcher, but away from him towards the dug-out where, traditionally, a bucket of refreshing water stood. It is not a stance that coaches encourage, yet again some great hitters have used it effectively, Roy Campanella, who is discussed on page 132, being one of them.

Among baseball's odder words is the 'fungo' which is a term for balls hit with a lighter than standard bat – a fungo stick – for fielding practice. There are also terms that apply to fielding. 'A can of corn' is a high fly ball that is easy to catch, and a 'charity hop' is when a driven ball bounces conveniently for the fielder concerned. A 'butcher' is another fielder's term and means not a hitter who destroys the pitching, but a fielder with a bad glove, a rarity. Another term of gore, a 'bleeder', is a hit that lands the hitter on first more by luck than good hitting. A bleeder bounces badly, or gets through the infield more by chance than good direction. A 'beanball', however, does imply gore even if it does not sound like it. A beanball is one aimed at a hitter's head to intimidate him. Beanballs can happen by accident, and can also happen deliberately, with the pitcher claiming they happen by accident. The penalty is not great, censure by the umpire, and since the early 1950s when Pittsburgh introduced helmets, beanballs became more and more frequent until the rules were strengthened. (Once, in 1920, a Yankee pitcher killed a Cleveland hitter with a beanball. History does not say if it was deliberate.) A pitcher who can 'bring it' is one with a consistently effective fast ball.

The man who uses this and other language successfully is known as a 'jockey', a player who is good at taunting the opposition from the dug-out bench, one of baseball's finer linguistic skills, because repetitive jockeys bore everyone. One has to be original to be a jockey. If the jockey goes too far with the umpire he is likely to be 'thumbed out', extracted from the game.

So much for slang. The other language in baseball is the official or semi-official language that you will need to understand commentators and to talk about the game. Here is a selection:

An Appeal, to be distinguished from an argument with the umpire, happens when the defensive team sees a breach in the rules by the offence, for example a player failing to touch the home plate or someone going to bat out of turn. There are certain such rules which demand an appeal, in other words it is up to the team offended against to bring them to the umpire's attention.

Assist is one of the forms of credit that fielders recieve. If, for example, a second baseman slows a hard hit ball so that it goes to the short stop and the short stop makes the out by throwing to first base, the second baseman is credited with the assist, for without his help the short stop would never have been able to make the out. The result is that assists tend to be credited to in- rather than outfielders, although if an outfielder makes a catch, then a runner runs and the outfielder throws to say, second base, as well as making the catch the outfielder has assisted second base in making the out.

Balk, or balking: one of the most complicated rules in baseball. Essentially it has to do with the pitcher failing to go through with the pitch once he is 'committed'. It is not, as many people think, a false move made by the pitcher before his foot is on the rubber, but after his foot is on the rubber, and there are thirteen different ways in which a balk can technically be called, the most common being a check after commitment to the pitch. The pitcher must also be stationary for a moment after bringing his hands down from the stretch. ('Stretch' and 'windup' are specific positions, one of which the pitcher must take before his delivery.)

Base On Balls is when a hitter reaches first base as a result of being thrown four balls, rather than by a hit.

Battery is a term that describes the pitcher and catcher as a unit.

The Box Score is the approved table that is essentially a complete record of the game. It looks like the example shown on p. 55.

The abbreviations in the box score are as follows:

In the upper columns:

The order of players is the batting order. Beside each player is his position, P for pitcher, this being a world series game played under National League rules. Therefore there is no DH, or designated hitter, but there is on either side a PH or pinch hitter (see later in this chapter).

Reading across the top, the batting part of the box score, the abbreviations are:

ab: at bat, number of times the individual came to bat.

r: runs, the number of runs scored, or the number of times the person ran home.

h: not home runs but the number of hits.

rbi: runs batted in. In other words if a player is at bat and hits into centre field with a runner on third, and the runner

CINCINNATI	ab	r	h	rbi	BOSTON	ab	r	h	rbi
Rose 3b	4	0	2	1	McEnaney p	0	0	0	0
Morgan 2b	4	0	2	1	Carbo lf	3	1	1	0
Bench c	4	1	0	0	Miller lf	0	0	0	0
Perez 1b	5	1	1	2	Beniquez ph	1	0	0	0
Foster lf	4	0	1	0	Doyle 2b	4	1	1	0
Concepcion ss	4	0	1	0	Montgomery ph	1	0	0	0
Griffey rf	2	2	1	0	Tastrzemski 1b	5	1	1	1
Geronimo cf	3	0	0	0	Fisk c	3	0	0	0
Gullett p	1	0	1	0	Lynn cf	2	0	0	0
Rettenmund ph	1	0	0	0	Petrocelli 3b	3	0	1	1
Billingham p	0	0	0	0	Evans rf	2	0	0	1
Armbrister ph	0	0	0	0	Burleson ss	3	0	0	0
Lee p	3	0	1	0	Moret p	0	0	0	0
Carroll p	0	0	0	0	Cooper ph	1	0	0	0
Driessen ph	1	0	0	0	Burton p	0	0	0	0
Willoughby p	0	0	0	0	Cleveland p	0	0	0	0
Total	33	4	0	4	Total	31	3	5	3

```
Cincinnati ............................................. 000 002 101—4
Boston................................................... 003 000 000—3
```

E—Doyle 2. DP—Cincinnati 1, Boston 2. LOB—Cincinnati 9, Boston 9, 2B—Carbo. HR—Perez (3). SB—Morgan, Griffey. S—Geronimo.

	IP	H	R	ER	BB	SO
Gullett	4	4	3	3	5	5
Billingham	2	1	0	0	2	1
Carroll (W. 1–0)	2	0	0	0	1	1
McEnaney	1	0	0	0	0	0
Lee	6½	7	3	3	1	2
Moret	⅓	1	0	0	2	0
Willoughby	1⅓	0	0	0	0	0
Burton (L. 0–1)	⅔	1	1	1	2	0
Cleveland	⅓	0	0	0	1	0

Save—McEnaney (1). WP—Gullett. T—2.52. A—35.205.

on third runs home safely, the latter is credited with an 'r', a run, while the person who made this possible is credited with an *rbi*, a run batted in.

Below the batting scores you will see the figures 000 002 101, each figure denoting the score in each inning, with the total at the end – 4 in this case.

Below that and above the pitching scores, the following abbreviations occur.

E for errors made by fielders or the pitcher when acting as a fielder, see later in this chapter.

DP for double plays, that is when two players are out in a single play, as already explained. A *TP* would be for a rare triple play.

LOB is the total number of men left on bases when the innings have ended.

2B has against it the number of two base hits. (In addition to hits that enable a batter to advance to second, generally a two base hit is given when the ball bounces out of the game, over the boundary.) There would also be *3B* had there been any three base hits.

HR is home runs, with the name of the player concerned. The (3) in brackets means that Perez has hit three home runs this season. Perez 2(4) would mean two home runs for this game, four for the season.

SB is for stolen bases.

S is for sacrifices, either fly balls or bunts, most commonly fly balls.

Then we come to the pitchers' part of the box score, somewhat confusing because the two sides are not separately tabulated, in this case Cincinnati names being featured first.

Reading across the column, the symbols mean as follows:

IP for innings pitched.

H for hits off that pitcher.

R for runs scored off that pitcher.

ER for earned runs off that pitcher. *R* and *ER* would only be different if one or more of the runs were made through errors by the fielders, in other words for reasons beyond the pitcher's control. If this happened the *ER* figure would be lower than the *R* figure. Next comes:

BB for bases reached on balls or walks.

SO for the number of strike outs.

The winning and losing pitchers are noted, these being the pitchers credited or debited with winning or losing, generally but not necessarily the starting pitchers.

Save: the pitcher credited with saving the game (see under 'Save' later in this chapter).

WP is not winning pitcher, but wild pitches (see later in this chapter).

T is the time taken to complete the game and *A* is for attendance.

Called Game is one ended by the umpire because of rain, snow, fog or wind. The rule is that the trailing team must go to bat five times for a game to be called, in other words it can be called any time after either the bottom or top of the fifth inning. If it is called after the top (first half) of the fifth, then the team due to bat in the bottom (second half) of the fifth inning must be leading.

Catcher's Interference, or sometimes catcher's error, is when the catcher interferes with the man at bat and the man at bat is given an automatic walk to first base. In addition if a man is attempting to steal during the interference, he is also allowed the extra base.

Count is the term used by commentators to state the number of balls and strikes, balls coming first. A 'count of three and two' means three balls and two strikes have been awarded against the particular man at bat.

A Cutoff is when a ball is intercepted as it is thrown in from the outfield and re-direted to prevent a man reaching base.

Dead Ball is a ball out of play because play has been suspended for interference or some other reason.

The Designated Hitter was introduced into the American

League in 1973, essentially to try to get more hitting into the game by removing the pitcher from the batting order. The designated hitter (who does not field) essentially substitutes at bat for the pitcher and can be placed at any point in the batting order. The device has proved somewhat controversial, but seems to be here to stay. American League batting scores are not noticably higher than those in the National League, where the pitcher has to hit.

Double is the term for a two base hit, and is noted in the box scores as we have seen above.

Double Header is two games in a series played one after the other (for the price of one).

Double Steal is when two base runners steal bases on the same play.

Earned Run; and Earned Run Average: An earned run is a run earned off a pitcher (rather than by a batter). If a run is scored on an error or obstruction, then it is not earned, and essentially the concept is one of counting successes against the pitcher.

The earned run average (ERA) is determined by dividing the total number of runs scored off a pitcher by the number of innings he has pitched, and then multiplying by nine. Thus if a pitcher goes for five innings and one run is scored off him, his ERA is one (run) divided by five (innings), which equals point two, multiplied by nine to make one point eight, the nine being the total number of innings in a game and the average being the average computed as if he had pitched throughout. An ERA of below three is considered good and the lowest ERA on record for three hundred innings or more in a season is that achieved in 1968 by Bob Gibson of the St Louis Cardinals: one point two.

Error is essentially a negative way of assessing fielders. An error is charged if a fielder fumbles or throws wild. An error is charged by the official scorer (not the umpire) when it leads to a batter having a longer time at bat, say if an error allowed a steal, or if it allows a runner to advance or a batter to reach base when he would not otherwise have done so. In professional baseball, the number of errors is generally very few, although it may not be when the fielding is aggressive, as in the 1986 World Series. However, one of the problems about beginning to watch professional baseball is that the fielding is so accurate it seems effortless a great deal of the time.

Fielder's Choice is when a fielder picks up a ground ball and decides to throw it other than to first. If, say, there is a runner on third and the short stop fields the ball, throwing it to the catcher rather than first base, then the man running from third to home plate is out on a fielder's choice.

Forfeit is rare and complex, but there are certain rules, for example if a team or player refuse to go on to the ground, the umpire can declare the game forfeited, giving a score of 9–0 to the team against whom the forfeit has been declared.

Foul Territory is that part of the playing field outside the third and first base lines.

To Ground Out is to hit a ground ball and be run out at first base.

Infield Fly is a fly ball that can be caught by an infielder with reasonable effort and which is hit when first, and second and/or first second and third bases are loaded and there are either no men out or only one man out.

If these seem rather complicated criteria, imagine a real situation: there are runners at first and second and no outs. An infield fly is hit, an easy catch for the pitcher. If he catches it, the man at bat is out. But if he drops it, the man at bat has to run and thereby forces the other base runners to do the same. In this case a double play is not difficult. The catcher throws to first and the first baseman throws to second, making two outs instead of the one if the catcher had caught the ball. That is why the rule says that the catcher (or the fielder to whom the ball is coming) must catch the ball. If the fielder drops the ball, then all runners automatically advance one base.

An infield fly is not, as would seem logical, a ball that falls within the geographical infield, but a ball that falls within what the umpire considers the normal reach of an infielder. It is not, says rule 2.00 'to be determined by some arbitrary limitation such as the grass or the base-lines.' It is also an infield fly if caught by an outfielder when, 'in the umpire's judgement, the ball could as easily have been handled by an infielder'.

One final point: an infield fly must be a fly ball, that is one hit high and looping off the top edge of the bat. The rule does not apply to dropped catches on either bunts or line drives.

Interference depends on who has interfered with whom. Offensive interference, says rule 2.00, 'is an act by the team at bat which interferes with, obstructs, impedes, hinders or confuses any fielder attempting to make a play'. The penalty is that the interfering player is out and any other runners go back to where they started from. Defensive interference is when fielders hinder or prevent the man at bat from hitting or prevent a runner from getting to a base. Umpire's interference is when he is hit by a ball that has not passed a fielder, or when he gets in the way of the catcher trying to prevent a stolen base. He rules as if there had been no interference and also does this if a spectator interferes, for example by leaning out of the stand and catching a ball in foul territory that a fielder would otherwise reasonably have caught. The ball is dead after interference.

A Line Drive is a ball hit hard and low which may or may not be caught.

A No Hitter is a game in which there are no hits and no runs scored.

An Overslide is when a man slides past base. A man running to first is home when he has touched the base and may run beyond, i.e. his momentum may allow him to keep going, but even if beyond the base he is not out if he has reached it before the ball has reached the first baseman with his foot on the base. But he must run across the foul line and away from, rather than towards, second. If he wavers for second and then changes his mind he can be tagged before returning to first.

And this rule applies to the other bases where the runner can be out if he overslides. Once at the base he is vulnerable if he goes beyond or over it. This is one reason why runners seldom slide or throw themselves into first but do so into other bases. Sliding means that the base itself acts as a brake for their momentum and keeps them attached and safe.

Passed Ball is a ball which the catcher fails to control *and* which results in a runner on base advancing. Also, if on the third strike the ball is hit, and would be going into foul territory were it not dropped by the catcher, it counts as a passed ball; and a passed ball is notched up as a catcher's error.

Pick Off is what a pitcher does when he catches a runner off base, and a 'good pick off motion' is what a pitcher is said to have when he is adroit at throwing to first to prevent steals. It is much easier for a left-handed pitcher to achieve this because he does not have to swing his whole body round in order to throw to first base. The term can also be applied to catchers, particularly in their ability to throw to second to prevent steals from first.

Pinch Hitter is a batter substituted for another, something which generally happens only in a 'pinch', towards the end of a game. Given the roster (see 'roster' p. 64) of twenty four men on the side, the manager can have as many pitchers and batters as he wants, but generally he has a pitching staff of about ten, which means that there are fourteen (as opposed to nine needed) on the hitting staff. Thus a good deal of substitution is theoretically possible, but in practice the use of pinch hitters tends to be minimal until the end of a game. In other words there may be a case in the eighth or ninth inning, for bringing in a pinch hitter to replace, say, a short stop who is not a strong hitter, but to do so earlier would deprive the side of a man chosen because his strength is as a short stop.

Another reason for bringing in a pinch hitter is that it may be thought that a right-handed pinch hitter is more effective than a left-handed player against a left-handed pitcher.

One of the puzzles of baseball is that some people seem to

be particularly successful as pinch hitters. Often they are either weak fielders, or hitters who are past the peak of their careers. But, when they come in to pinch hit, there is expectation from the crowd and they seem to get it just right, scoring a home run or allowing runners to advance who are already on base. In 1932, for example, Johnny Frederick hit six pinch hit home runs for the Brooklyn Dodgers, each of which clinched the game. Two years running, in 1958 and 1959, a Philadelphia pinch hitter made hits nine times in a row, incredible when one thinks that .400 hits per time at bat is exceptional for the best batters. And another player, Joe Morales, once made twenty five pinch hits in a row for Montreal during a season.

A Pinch Runner is not dissimilar to a pinch hitter. The rule says that a runner may be substituted for a man on base, and this sometimes happens if the man on base is a slow runner or cannot run at full tilt because of an injury. But the player taken out may not play again in that game, and it is a tactical device that is seldom used before the eighth or ninth inning. For example, in a tied ninth inning, a substitute short stop who was very agile might be used to pinch run for a big hitter who was slow and was standing at second. The big hitter could not be used again in the game anyway, so nothing is lost by the device.

Platoon is the device of using two different players for one position, generally a right- and left-handed hitter at a certain point in the batting order. There is a long running argument among baseball statisticians about whether right-handed batters score better against left-handed pitchers, etc. The difficulty with the statistics is that while they suggest that hitters of average ability do better against pitchers of the opposite hand, the great players belie the argument. Reggie Jackson, Babe Ruth, Joe DiMaggio, Hank Aaron, etc. never needed to be platooned. For a time in the early part of the century the practice became fashionable, but has not been used systematically in recent years except by the manager

Charles Dillon Stengal, alias Casey Stengal, alias Casey, one of the best loved figures in baseball. Casey was in turn manager of the Brooklyn Dodgers, Boston Braves, New York Yankees and New York Mets during the 'forties and early 'fifties winning seven World Series in twelve years. It was his practice to use platooning extensively, both defensively and aggressively, in other words he used the device to throw off another team's pitching plans. Clearly it worked for him; either this was a fluke, or others do not quite know the trick.

Quick Pitch is one thrown hurriedly to put a batter off balance and in the hope that the umpire will not notice. If he does it is a balk (see p. 54) and all players on bases advance one. If there are no players on bases, it counts simply as a ball.

Relief Pitcher is one who comes in to replace another; there may be two or more relief pitchers in any one game.

Relief pitchers fall into three categories to match three different kinds of ability:

A 'mop-up' man is not quite what he sounds, but an inexperienced pitcher who is given a chance at relief when the outcome of a game is virtually certain.

A 'long man' is a relief pitcher who comes in early in the game if the starter (or starting pitcher) is in trouble. Quite often a long man will be another starting pitcher and contrasts strongly with:

A 'short man', alias the fireman, someone who can pitch extremely well under difficult circumstances, usually with his team behind, and keep his nerve.

Why some pitchers should be better as starters and others as relievers is, fundamentally, a mystery. It is partly a matter of temperament, for starters have to be consistent over many pitches, partly of the kind of stamina that a particular pitcher has. Most pitchers fall into one category or another fairly soon in their career.

Resin Bag is an approved bag of resin that is always placed at the back of the pitcher's mound, and may be used for making his fingers slightly sticky, although it may not be applied directly to the ball. (Pitchers frequently will try to apply other sticky substances to the ball to improve its flight: saliva, hair tonic, petroleum jelly etc. Myth has it that pitchers often get away with this, something umpires deny, but the truth is probably that pitchers do this less often than may be thought. On one occasion a pitcher was forced to shampoo between innings because the umpire was convinced that he was putting grease hidden in his hair onto the ball.)

The Roster is the official number of players on the side. It is now twenty-four, down from twenty-five, essentially to save money. Generally it consists of nine pitchers, five starters and four relievers with a mixture of right- and left-handers and a mixture of 'long' and 'short' men, pitchers who are most effective over a large or small number of innings. There will always be a spare infielder on the roster, preferably a versatile one, able to field in any of the positions, and there will always be a spare catcher, for catchers are particularly prone to injury. And there will probably be someone who is an effective pinch hitter.

Between the end of the minor league season early in September and the start of the play offs, the roster can be increased from twenty-four to forty players, allowing major league teams to bring minor league players from their associated or 'farm' teams before making their final choices, should they be in the play-offs.

Runs Batted In, RBIs, or sometimes 'ribbies' are the statistics most coveted by hitters, even more than hits. An RBI is credited to the man at bat when he makes a hit that takes a runner home. It does not matter whether the man at bat is out after making the hit, either by being caught or by being put out at a base, it is still to his credit. For the most important thing in baseball is not to hit but to score, and RBIs have been described by one American sportswriter, Zander Hollander, as 'the lifeblood of the offense'.

A Save is the credit given to a relief pitcher who finishes a game and keeps a lead established by another pitcher, or wins a game after being in a losing situation. The rules for granting a save to a pitcher are complex but they are essentially:

If there is a lead of no more than three, then he must pitch at least one inning, or. . . .

He must pitch at least three innings and protect a lead, or . . .

If there is a lead of one, the potential tying run must either be scored by a man already on base or by one of the first two men to whom he pitches.

Shutout is when a team fails to score in a game. (A perfect game, on the other hand, is when a pitcher fails to let a single batter advance to a single base, and pitches the whole game.)

Squeeze Play is when a team has a runner at third and less than two out. The man at bat tries to advance the man at third by means of a bunt.

A Starting Pitcher has to be declared to the umpire before the game. Once in the game he must finish pitching to at least one player, unless injured.

A Suspended Game is one where the umpire calls off play, but is different from a called game (see p. 57). Games are rarely suspended; essentially the only reason would be that the sun was coming up and the players and umpires too exhausted to continue.

One famous minor league game between the Red Sox team who are based in Rhode Island, the Pawtucket Red Sox, and the Rochester Red Wings, was thus suspended after thirty-two innings. The game began on April 18, 1981 and continued until 4.05 a.m. on the next morning, Easter morning and bitterly cold. The score had been 1–1 at the end of nine innings. In the twenty-second innings, as fate would have it, each side scored one. Normally such a game would have been called off at 1 a.m., but the umpires claimed that the rule book issued by the International (minor) League, did not contain this curfew law. Eventually appeals to the League President called off the game. It was restarted on the next visit of

Rochester to Pawtucket several weeks later, and was quickly won by the Pawtucket Red Sox in front of the world's press.

To Take a pitch is not, as it sounds, to swing at it but to do the opposite, to let a pitch go without hitting at it.

Wild Pitch is a pitch thrown so wide or high of the plate that it cannot be caught by the catcher, and results in a runner advancing a base. If there is no runner on base, it does not count as a wild pitch, but if a runner does move up, then it is charged on the pitcher's official chart not as an error, simply as a wild pitch. It seldom happens in the majors, and should not be confused with 'wasting' a pitch, which is when the pitcher, with the count in his favour, throws a ball deliberately a bit wide to tempt the batter into coming out and hitting it as a flyball.

Windup is one of two legal positions being allowed to the pitcher before making his delivery, the other being the 'set' position as defined in the rules, more commonly known as the 'stretch'. Essentially the stretch is a shorter windup than the full windup position, and is used as a way of preventing runners on base from taking too big a lead, and thereby stealing. The rules about the windup and stretch positions are highly technical and if not obeyed constitute a balk by the pitcher. However, there are those who argue that umpires are generally lax in terms of exact enforcement. For example a footnote to rule 8.01(b) emphasises that: 'the pitcher, following his stretch, must (a) hold the ball in both hands in front of his body and (b) come to a complete stop'. The footnote goes on: 'this rule must be enforced. Pitchers are constantly attempting to "beat the rule" in their efforts to hold runners on bases.'

THE REAL THING:
BOSTON AND NEW YORK IN
THE WORLD SERIES

For me as a fan it was a dream come true. I had followed the Boston Red Sox for seven years of complicated emotions for a team that never quite came together, a team that would always do the wrong thing, win against people who should defeat them, lose against people whom they should have beaten, go into unpredictable slumps and then have equally unpredictable points of shining brilliance. Over the years I watched them, Boston fielding was always strong, and the double plays spectacular. Boston hitting was pretty good. Boston pitching was brilliant occasionally but generally not good enough, too erratic. Then, in 1985, a tall young right-hander from Texas joined the team, Roger Clemens. He was injured for much of that year with a shoulder problem, and there were questions about his future. But as the 1986 season matured, Boston went into the lead and Clemens did a lot to put them there. They added strength elsewhere, but somehow this player had the effect of making them win and making them win made them better. Nothing succeeds like success.

There was one very bad moment. At the beginning of July is the All Star game, when players from the two Leagues play each other. Clemens was chosen as the lead-off pitcher for the American League and another Boston pitcher, Dennis 'Oil Can' Boyd was not chosen at all. Boyd, only twenty-three, was known to be temperamental and had shown the strains stardom imposed on someone from the poorest and most remote part of rural Mississippi. During a game before the All Stars, he walked out, was found sulking by the press, said the wrong things, apologized to his team mates in a way they thought was grudging, then got into a scuffle with the police, went off to a hospital in Central Massachusetts with accusations of drug taking being fired off from all fronts, then disappearing like puffs of smoke. Coincidentally with the Oil Can saga, or possibly because of it, the Red Sox went to pieces on a long road tour, and a large lead in the League became minimal. Paranoia hit the team and the Boston press. The Red Sox were going to do it again, 'it' being to throw away in the last half of the season everything they had gained in the first. I was in Massachusetts at the time and talk of this was everywhere, in the press, on television, muddled in with the main news, on talk shows, women's shows, cooking shows. Turn on the radio in the car, or look at television at night, read the paper in the morning: it was impossible to avoid seeing or hearing someone in Massachusetts voicing the final opinion on the matter. I suppose it is a measure of how much baseball matters to people, but it seemed a rather debased one as this young and brilliant, if sometimes arrogant, player was in trouble.

Greatly to his credit and the dignity of the sport he pulled himself together, dropped or tried to drop the 'Oil Can' and became just Dennis Boyd, talented and maturing pitcher. Boston led the eastern division at the end of the season, then came back from 3–1 down to win the American League pennant against California, only the sixth team in history to have done this. They were in the World Series.

The opposition were the powerful New York Mets, who had led eastern division of the National League with an ease that few teams over the years have been able to afford. So when in New York, on a balmy October Saturday evening, Boston beat them in the first game, it was something of a surprise. Boston were very much the underdogs and the New York papers had talked about the series going to the Mets 4–0.

For the first seven innings of the first game there was no score. Then Darling threw a fast ball low and to the right of the Boston right hander, Dwight Evans. Evans did not swing at the pitch, which was clearly a ball; the Mets' catcher put out his gloved hand, the ball hit it, skewed fast to the left between the catcher and Evans and the catcher went sprawling as he dived to pick it up. By the time he had recovered the ball, Jim Rice, already on first base, was at second. He had advanced on a catcher's error.

The situation looked not unfavourable for Boston but then Evans was run out on a ground ball, with Rice still at second. In came Gedman, the Boston catcher. He struck the ball hard and along the ground to the Mets' second baseman, who could and should have caught it clean to put Gedman out at first and put Boston out, scoreless. By an extraordinary error, the kind of error you do not expect from the Mets, the ball eluded him, speeding backwards to centre field.

We were to see a beautiful bit of running by Rice, who is by no means fast. On the assumption that the side would be out if the ball was fielded and that a double play running him out would achieve nothing, Rice was going before the ball was hit, stealing. The signal from the third base coach was quick and direct so that half-way to third Rice was being called around it, could begin to veer outwards in order to take the corner more easily and continue his momentum to home plate.

69

When the throw came in it coincided with his slide to the plate, but to make the catch, the catcher had to move forward a yard ahead of the plate and Rice was in.

Points to notice: great teams do make errors occasionally. Rice's run was a close thing, and he would not have scored had he not run so well and co-ordinated so well with the third base coach. Gedman might have gone to second, but he stayed at first. Had he gone to second he might have been run out, and the side would have been retired, with Rice still not at home plate.

Another point: there is an expression about teams which says that they are 'strong up the middle', or have 'a strong spine'. This is based on the fact that most vulnerable area from a fielding point of view is up the middle, around second base and short stop. As there is often a trade-off between fielding and batting ability, the stronger a team is at batting, the more it can afford second basemen and short stops who may have little batting ability. A team with a weaker batting order would not be able to afford the luxury. The Mets are a team that has been described as particularly strong up the middle. But not this time. The run was to give Boston the first game.

On the Monday, for the second game, two of the outstanding young pitchers in the country faced each other: Dwight Gooden for the Mets, Roger Clemens for Boston Red Sox. When I saw him in 1984 as a rookie, Gooden was extraordinary, being put forward by some enthusiasts as the best pitcher ever. By 1986 his devastating strike-out rate had declined a bit, but he was still considered as good a pitcher as there was, on the best team.

Nothing happened until the top (first half) of the third inning, or rather a lot of good pitching happened, much of which we were not shown by Channel Four, but very little hitting. The first man up was Spike Owen, the Boston short stop, whose batting average was only .231. He was to be followed by Clemens, who never bats at all in the American

League. It did not look like a difficult inning for Gooden, just a matter of polishing off the bottom of the Red Sox order.

The first pitch was a ball, the second a strike. The third was a fast ball to which Owen got the end of his bat and hit foul to the left. So the 'count' was one–two, one ball, two strikes. The next was a ball, two–two. Then came a change of pace, a strongly breaking pitch, but that was a ball too, three and two. Once again a change of pace, a fast ball, very low, almost hitting the plate. Four–two. Owen walked. A pitcher like Gooden should never walk a hitter of Owen's weakness. Boggs or Rice or Evans, yes, but not Owen.

Clemens then did the only thing he could do – bunt; wise, because even if he sacrificed, Owen as a shortstop is very fast and had a chance of making second. The bunt was not skilful in the first part of its operation. The pitcher could see his opponent's hands moving down the bat's shaft before the windup was completed, but Clemens did connect. The Mets' first baseman, Hernandez had come right in, predicting the bunt, fielded it just in front of the pitcher, but then threw it clumsily to second so that it bounced, and bounced out of the hand of the Mets' second baseman.

Points to notice: the bunt was clearly the right tactic, but should Hernandez have moved in so far so early? If he had not done so, the pitcher could have fielded it just as well and thrown Clemens out at first (where Hernandez should have been) and Hernandez might then have made it a double play by throwing Owen out at second. They should certainly have had one out. Instead they had none, two men on base and the return to the top of the Boston order.

Another point to notice: this World Series produced a high number of errors. This could be put down to nervousness on the parts of the players – who would not be nervous with seventy-thousand dollars in personal fee at stake? – but seems to have had more to do with the tight character of the Series itself. The fielding throughout was aggressive – the term used by the commentator was 'fast and loose'. This created a paradoxical situation, because the faster fielding, the more likely fielders are to make mistakes. In other words if it is fast it is also likely to be, on occasion, loose. Fielding conservatively is easier, but does not necessarily make for getting every extra inch out of a game.

Boggs came to bat next and the pitch was elegant and fast. Boggs did not move. The next one he hit foul, so that the count was nought and two. But Boggs has an un-nerving (for pitchers) record in nought and two positions, the kind of record that makes him a very great hitter indeed. And that was confirmed on the next pitch, again straight and fast, very tricky..

Boggs could not let this go, because that would be the third strike. But clearly he felt he could not get right behind it lest he pop the ball up. So he hit it, right at the last moment, almost 'out of the catcher's glove' as the commentator put it, up high and left, but foul. It was what is called a 'protective swing', deliberately hitting the ball foul when the count is against a batter, and it is something which required such timing as very few players have ever posessed. Boggs then got on top of the next pitch, much the same type of delivery and much the same type of hit. This one was not protective, but a well-timed drive over third base, landing just inside the foul line, bouncing out and then in again, but always in play because it bounced before it crossed the foul line. With this Owen ran in, Clemens went to third and Boggs to first.

True, I am a Red Sox fan. But this was baseball at its most dramatic – two stolid innings and a third where the side should have been polished off. Instead of that Boston were in a very strong position.

Another point to notice: American League hitters seldom play against National League pitchers, so what the systematic Boggs does is to analyse the pitcher in his own League closest to Gooden in style, rhythm and mood, in this case a Seattle pitcher he often faces. Boggs has an aide who works out all the statistics for him, and he develops his evening's performance from there. Indeed among major league players he is probably the most systematic in this way. He even insists on eating a particular dish of chicken cooked in a particular way and in a particular portion at a set time before each game. It may sound obsessive, but it seems to work. And baseball players become great by recognizing what works for them, whether it is a certain way of swinging at certain balls, or their diet or exercise regime.

Barrett came in next, and Barrett too upset Gooden, hitting a strong single that allowed Clemens to run in and Boggs to go to third. Boston were then two up. Short and stolid, Barrett – a second baseman who has become a very strong hitter – was followed by Buckner, who reached for the second pitch and hit it low off the bat into right field, very hard, breaking the bat and running Boggs home. After that Gooden got back into his stride and Boston were retired, 3–0 ahead. But not for long.

Clemens now faced Santana, the short stop and number eight in the Mets' order and a potentially easy out for Clemens. But, as when Clemens himself was batting, the call went to two and three, two balls, two strikes, before Santana hit the pitch hard up the middle. Clemens jumped and reached for the ball, failed to make the play off the bounce in front of him, which could have resulted in an easy out at first. Instead Owen, the short stop, fielded it but misdirected the throw (which still should have produced an easy out) to the Boston first baseman's feet instead of his glove, causing him to move off the plate. So the Mets had one on with no outs.

Now it was Clemens' turn to deal with the Mets' pitcher, and as Clemens had done, the pitcher bunted. As the Mets had done, the Boston first baseman came in very close. The hit was a little looping pop up, Buckner the first baseman threw himself headlong at it, had it *on* his glove but not *in* his glove, and it went loose. The Mets had two men on bases, no outs, and were back at the top of the order. Such a symmetrical pattern of play is rare in baseball.

Suddenly Boston's lead looked vulnerable, and the whole

73

infield met on the mound to try to set up a defensive play. It seems to have worked. Dykstra, the Mets' lead-off man, instead of trying to hit over the close infield, bunted, but too hard, the bane of all bunting. Boggs at third base fielded very quickly, threw Dykstra out at first, but left runners at second and third. An uncomfortable situation for Boston, and more uncomfortable when Backman hit a hard ground ball that took him to first and ran in Santana, a notorious stealer, leaving Gooden on third.

It looked good for the Mets, but then came two astonishing pieces of fielding, both by Boggs, running out in turn the next two men in the order. So the Red Sox held on to their lead, but only just, three–two.

In the fourth inning Boston increased the lead by one, a huge home run into centre field by Henderson, a hit that the television commentator said must have come down with icicles attached to it – a good description of the height of hit, even if it did not quite allow for the physics of friction heating the ball up on the return to earth. That put Boston up four to two. But in the bottom of the fourth the Mets made two hits, each within a handful of feet of the right field boundary, both to be caught, but both potential home runs in parks smaller than Shea, although not at Boston which has almost the same dimensions on the right.

In the fifth the first man up for Boston was Rice, who for the second time in the game hit a ground ball and put himself on first. The next man up was Dwight Evans, who hit a homer into left field, putting Boston ahead six–two. In the bottom of the fifth there was another astonishing piece of Boston fielding, Evans flinging himself sideways for a high fast ball deep into right field and just keeping the ball above ground in the top of his glove, a catch that involved him using his left (gloved) hand while running very fast to the right, the kind of catch that happens once in ten games.

But in spite of this one out, Clemens soon had runners on first and third. A lead of four is big, but not so big against the heart of the Mets' batting order. Clemens was relieved and Crawford came in to pitch for Boston, varying his pitches more than Clemens and striking out Strawberry. Two out, two on bases. Better for Boston, but not good. And worse when Heep hit Crawford for a single, thereby 'loading the bases'. Not good at all, and just the kind of change of fortune that makes baseball, arguably, a very fast game. Now the Mets runners were ready to go. But instead came the anticlimax. The count was three and two, three balls, two strikes but the next ball Johnson hit to the short stop, who fielded cleanly, threw to first and put him out.

It would be hard to imagine three more tense innings in baseball, such a combination of hitting and scoring, three bunts, two pieces of exceptional fielding, a surprisingly large number of errors, a lot of variation in fielding tactics, two of the best pitchers around badly unseated. After two games Boston were two up.

Game three was in Boston, with Boyd pitching after a marvellous recent record. But then in the first inning, on the count of one and one, Dykstra hit him for a home run. On the count of three and one Backman, number two in the Mets' order, hit him for a single. Boyd skilfully held Backman down at first base, and stopped him trying to steal, but the next man at bat, Hernandez, hit him deep into left field, and so did the next man, Carter, allowing Backman to score. In the top of the first inning Boston were down two–nought with two men on base and not a single out.

Boyd did strike out the next man, Strawberry, but then came a very odd fielding situation.

Ray Knight was batting with runners at second and third. The pitch was a good one, lower than Knight expected. He just caught it with the end of the bat and the ball bounced to Boggs at third base who fielded it clean. The runner at third made for the plate, but by the time that Boggs had thrown he had retreated, making back for third, so that the catcher now had to throw it to third.

75

Meanwhile the runner from second had advanced to third, so there were two runners making for third. The catcher did what he could and threw the ball to Boggs who had come forward. He tried to tag the runner going back to third in mid-run but missed him, and by the time he got the ball to the short stop at third the runner had got back. The short stop then tried to chase the runner going back to second, but failed to catch him and threw the ball to second, but the runner who had been on second got back there too.

And there was so much confusion that Knight, who had hit the ball, was by this time comfortably on first.

You do not see runners tagged out often in major league baseball. But this was a case of a very badly missed opportunity by Boston. The Mets were not in a force play situation. In other words, because there was no runner on first, there was no need for those on second and third to advance on the hit. But the Mets are an aggressive team and an aggressive team here with a lead. Boston seemed to have forgotten that and, in doing so, missed the rare opportunity for a triple play.

The game did not seem to be going Boston's way, although they did go on to score one in the third. But at the end of the sixth, the Mets again looked dangerous. When Carter came in to bat the bases were loaded and there were two outs. Boyd was still pitching, in the circumstances a sign of managerial faith. The first pitch to Carter was a strike. So was the second: nought and two. Would this be the last pitch and hold the Mets down?

The pitch was straight, but Carter hit hard into left. One man ran home and a second took the chance, which paid off as the throw was wild. The Boston catcher then threw to second, to which Carter appeared to be running. But as soon as the throw went, Carter reversed, going back to first. The second baseman then threw to first, at which point Carter reversed again, going back to second. Finally he was tagged before he reached second, but once again here was a good example of a runner using his head in a difficult situation. Or should he have been content to stay on first? If he had done so, the situation, already bad for Boston, now 6–1 down, would have become positively ugly. As it was Carter was out, the Mets retired – but went on to win seven–one.

Anything can happen in World Series baseball. But when a team scores as early as the Mets did in this game, it can be very hard to beat. Scoring off a fresh pitcher can be devastating psychologically, and puts the manager in a quandary. He has only so many pitchers to call on. He has several more games to go. If he rotates too early he is drawing on valuable resources. If he does not rotate he may be holding on to a pitcher on an off night, as this clearly was for Oil Can Boyd.

In the fourth game the score was nought–nought until the fourth inning, when there was an interesting example of what is called 'protecting the runner'. There was a runner at first and Hernandez was at bat. Almost certainly the sign to steal on a particular pitch was made. Whether the Red Sox pitcher knew this or not, the pitch was way off the strike zone. Hernandez was desperate to hit it, reached right out, so far out that he lost his grip on the bat. Normally a hitter would have let this go as a ball – another example of the intensity the World Series produces. But the sacrifice worked, and although Hernandez was easily put out at first, second was taken by the runner. It did not, in fact, make much difference because the next pitch was hit for a glorious, over the wall home run, which put the Mets two ahead. They then scored another run in that inning to go three ahead.

By the end of the fifth the score was still Mets three, Boston two, although in three different innings Boston had two men stranded on base failing to score in any of them. It seemed that Darling, the Mets' pitcher, was just that much more on top than the Boston pitchers, Nipper and Hurst, eroding Boston each inning with his pitches, striking men out or forcing them to 'pop up', that is to hit high, catchable fly balls. It is not an easy thing to see this, but in professional baseball, the game always takes place on the margin, and understanding or speculating on the particular nature of this margin is what makes baseball such an intense pleasure to those who know the game. All through this World Series so far, scores had been made not just by straight hits but by fielding errors, creative running and quick thinking by the runners, and by always taking advantage of the occasional loose pitch. In other words, you could say of the series so far that there had been some great hitting, but you could equally well say that the good hitting had come when the pitchers provided the opportunities.

Later on, in game four, the lead expanded. The Mets won six to two and the series was now tied, two games each.

No one had yet won at home, but in game five Boston were to do so. An analysis highlights once again this point about the margins. Twice the Mets' outfield were deceived by hits deep into left field. On one Strawberry (the right fielder) missed the bounce against the bull-pen wall, on the second Dykstra did the same thing, being fooled by a ball sailing around in the wind, a little like a sliced ball in golf.

In each case Boston reached an extra base off the hit, and in each case the extra base was to contribute to the run. But it was also interesting to see how very close Strawberry and Dykstra were to each other when each made his respective mistake, one there to help the other. Most backing up of this kind in fielding is unnecessary, but it is worth watching for among the very great teams. They always back up very closely, even when the play is an easy one. And there is a famous case when on a high, easy catch to left field, to everyone's surprise the left fielder fumbled the ball. It jumped out of his glove and one of the most surprised was the centre fielder, Pete Rose, who was, out of instinct, just a few feet away. Rose caught the ball.

So Boston won game five, four/two, the first home game to be won, and it put them in the lead when they went back to New York for Game six. Throughout the swing of fortune seemed to be going their way.

In game six, Boston scored one in the first and then another. Then the Mets scored one and then another. Then Boston scored again and then the Mets scored again. At the beginning of the ninth inning it was three:three. In the top of the ninth Boston failed to score. The game was tied. Then in the tenth Knight, one of the weakest Mets' hitters, walked to first. Wilson bunted and Knight ran for second. Gedman, the Boston catcher, retrieved the ball and threw it to second with Knight diving for the base. It looked as if Knight was out but the umpire called him safe.

On to the field came the Red Sox manager, fuming and cursing and abusing the umpire. Barratt and Gedman were also sure Knight was out, but on a replay you could see what happened. Barratt had to jump to catch the throw from Gedman, and in doing so his foot left the base without the ball in his glove, and came down on to the base again with it. In the intervening few frames of video, perhaps a quarter of a second, the runner touched the base with outstretched arms. The umpire knew he was right, and took a lot of abuse with patience.

Things then went from bad to worse for Boston, but they were helped by a call with the next man at bat. The count on pitches was one and two, one ball, two strikes. The next pitch was high, but the batter moved and, muct to his disgust, the umpire called a checked swing. (The rule for checked swing says that if the man at bat swings and then checks this counts as a swing.) He was out, and Boston were now in a slightly better position with one Mets' man out and two on bases.

In fact the next Mets' hitter was out too, caught. The pendulum seemed to be swinging further in Boston's favour. Once again the plate umpire called a checked swing, but this time the third base umpire over-ruled him, another sign of very good umpiring, as a less experienced or more prickly plate umpire might not have accepted the over-ruling. The tension rose with two men out and a count of two and nought, two balls, no strikes. The Mets needed only one run to win the game and tie up the series. Boston, having been in a position to win for most of this last game, now needed to make no mistakes. Nor did they. Carter mistimed a pitch and struck a looping ball into the hands of Jim Rice. The Mets were out, the game tied at the end of ten innings.

But almost immediately Henderson hit a home run for Boston, a wonderful smashing drive into left field, a run of which he was so confident that he danced at the plate before moving, then ran back a few steps and then round the bases. The Mets struck out the next two men, but then Boggs came to bat, hit a double and once again with a 'full count' (two outs, three balls, two strikes) Barratt hit the ball hard enough to run Boggs in.

When the Mets came to the bottom of the eleventh, they were therefore two runs down, with the score Boston five, Mets three. It was an ugly situation for any team, even though the Mets had come from behind to win thirty-nine times in the regular season. Almost immediately Carter got to first. Then, with two outs, the Mets had men on first and second. Boston then changed pitcher and in came Stanley, who is essentially a reliever, and a vicious one, best in this kind of last minute situation. The count went to one and one and then Stanley threw a ball hard and low and wild. The catcher failed to reach it, the runner came home, the next ball against Stanley was misfielded at first – it appeared that Bill Buckner, the Boston first baseman, thought it was going to the foul line side of the base. But on a replay his failure to field was almost inexplicable. His error was displayed across the nation and only gradually did it emerge that he was playing with a broken bone in his leg and was simply incapable of bending in the right direction. Playing him was therefore a very controversial piece of management. Boston had lost the sixth game five to six and the series was tied and victory for the first time since 1918 snatched out of the hands of Boston. There is always a risk with pitchers of such extreme strength as Stanley and Boston had fallen foul of taking that risk.

In the final, rain-delayed, game, Boston were beaten, as three million British viewers know. Or, put differently, the Mets won. In fact that seems to be the positive way to put it. My dreams were shattered, although by long before this is read I will have started dreaming again. The fact is that the Mets were just slightly better. Boston's recovery in the first half of the tenth inning of the sixth game was remarkable. The Mets recovery was more so. Boston's lead in the early part of the seventh game was the result of very good baseball. But the Mets ploughed on. Errors had been made by both sides, both sides pitchers at times failed to live up to expectation, men were left on base by both sides. But, in the final resort this was a world series in which life (hitting) triumphed over death (pitching). The pitching was about even, and the Mets hitting was just that much better. The seven acts makes it more like Wagner's 'Ring' than a normal drama. But it would have been hard to find a more exciting World Series. Everyone supports a team. But finally they have to support the only thing larger than the teams, the game itself.

9

MORE ON PITCHERS
AND PITCHING

Black neither responded nor changed his expression.
He simply threw one fast ball each at the heads of
Cincinnati's next seven batters. 'Musta been some
crooners in that lot', he said. 'That stopped the
music'.

From Roger Kahn's *The Boys of Summer*

The rhythm of a pitcher's playing life varies between not
pitching most of the time, then having to do so with an
intensity that is about as great as that endured by any player
in any sport.

The mound is a lonely place. The pitcher is prince out there
on the sandy hillock, but the prince carries a great burden. He
knows that he has the advantage, that it is very difficult for
anyone to hit his pitches. He knows too that all eyes are upon
him, and perfect games being rare, he will be judged more by
his mistakes than his accomplishments. The hungry animal
of baseball feeds on hits. In the silent hours players will be
dissecting his every move, analyzing his figures, his combination of fast and slower balls, the rhythm of his deliveries,
his ability to change pace. He must destroy this analysis, and
in the process he will risk destroying himself too. A pitcher's
arm is so sore after a six inning stint at the mound that most

starting pitchers require four days off between appearances.

Pitchers inflict pain on the aspirations of their opposition. They also suffer pain. Good pitching involves ninety-two mile an hour fast balls. Great pitching comes when the speed increases to ninety-five, but in that two or three per cent extra lies the danger zone, of wildness, of counts going bleakly against, of walks to the mound by the emperor manager. Crowds appreciate pitching, but appreciate hitting the more. A pitcher may have done great things to hold a side down to a two run lead, but he will not get the kind of cheers that accompany a home run.

One of the best modern books on pitching, indeed on baseball, is by Jim Brosnan, about the 1961 season when he was the most successful Cincinnati pitcher and helped them win the World Series. The book includes pitching records which show that Brosnan, pitching in more games than any of the other ten Cincinnati pitchers, nevertheless pitched in only fifty-three or less than one in three throughout the season. Most of the pitching staff pitched in between twenty and thirty games, in other words rather less than once a week did they go to the mound at all. The most innings pitched by a Cincinnati pitcher – typical of a professional side in this regard – was two hundred and forty-six, or about ten a week. To pitch well involves a lot of time not pitching, and that is as good a measure as any of the necessary concentration.

Pitching quite well, or quite fast, or making the ball break a certain amount is not difficult for a major league pitcher. The difficulty comes with pitching to the ultimate degree of concentration and physical effort. How difficult it is can be seen by looking at the number of pitches that go awry when one of the best pitchers is at the mound. Sometimes he will get strike after strike, but a lot of time the count will go to two and two, two balls, two strikes. The balls may be deliberate, of course, tactics in leading on the man at bat, but a lot are simply off kilter. If you get a chance to record television baseball, freeze a frame just a moment after the ball has left

84

the pitcher's hand. You will not see an expression of easy satisfaction. You will see a face contorted. Every muscle in the body has been used and on the face you will see more than determination. You will see pain.

The action of the pitcher is best described as a whiplash. He starts with his weight behind the rubber, raises the ball high in both hands as he begins to bring his weight forward, lowers them, brings the weight forward onto the rubber and then whips his whole body forward, legs, hips, shoulders and finally pitching arm as he delivers. There are many different styles in the body action of the pitcher, particularly – or most noticeably – in how far the front leg is taken up in the air, in the case of some pitchers as high as the head, forcing the body and centre of gravity backwards before the body goes through the whip line action of the delivery. You will also notice that some pitchers throw with their arm more to the side, some with their arm higher up. This is partly a matter of individual style and partly a matter of arm action, of where the strain is being taken between shoulders, elbow and wrist, something that determines the type of pitch delivered, or the way the ball moves in the air. Most pitchers now are over-arm or side-arm, propelling the ball when their arms are extended at right angles to the body or higher. Under-arm pitchers are few and far between in any of the professional leagues, but there is one worth noting, Quisenberry of Kansas City, who says he got tired of throwing over-arm. For all that he is one of the new laid-back generation of pitchers, Quisenberry is devastating as a reliever, a destroyer who eschews the height the mound gives him and throws from somewhere opposite his trouser pocket. He is pretty, more like a fast armoured car in appearance than a Sherman tank.

The pitcher's armoury of different deliveries is as follows:

Fast Balls (although as has been noted before this is something of a confusing term. All pitches in professional baseball are fast.)

85

Fast balls are essentially thrown with the first two fingers either across the seam or along it. In other words there is no interference from the fingers as in more elaborate spinning balls. And the wrist must not be moved or twisted. Thrown thus it can also be made to sink. A **Sinker** is a kind of fast ball. Or it can rise, depending on the height of the pitcher's arm. So even a fast ball moves in two directions, forwards and up or down after a certain point in its flight.

To understand what a baseball pitcher is doing, try playing ducks and drakes with flat stones. You spin the stone in various ways and you will find that it moves in various ways in its flight before hitting the water, as it looses speed and as air currents build up around it. To do this with a non-spherical object thrown at about thirty miles an hour is not difficult, although to determine the direction in which you want the stone to turn, is. Essentially this is what a pitcher is doing, with a spherical object whose only irregularity is in the seams. He is spinning the ball in a particular way and driving it with his arm in a particular way, so that as the air currents build up in relation to the ball's momentum, so it will turn in the air in one plane or another.

Curve Balls have to be thrown with a side-arm pitch. Or rather if thrown 'overhand' – that is with the arm high like a bowler in cricket – the curve will tend to 'break down'. Spin will not be implemented, at least in most hands. (Remember though that as with batters, many of the great pitchers are the exception to any rules of action.) By having the arm at three-quarter height there is tension on the elbow which is kept up, – tension which is lost if the arm is held too high. The curve essentially comes from the way the ball leaves the hand, or rather the middle finger of the hand, and from the flick of the wrist which is started before the ball is released and finished as a follow through.

Sliders are essentially fast balls that curve, or that break sharply late in their trajectory, the difference between them and curve balls being that they are faster and break later

86

and more sharply. One method of teaching sliders is to instruct the pitcher to give a back spin to a fast ball, simultaneously turning the hand. But there are various methods, in all of which the hand must be brought down across the body.

The effectiveness and direction of sliders depend very much on the right/left hand relationship between pitcher and batter. Thus they may break towards or away from the batter, and may also rise or sink, generally the latter as this cuts the ball downwards across the batter's swing. The ball may break upwards as well, so that it is breaking both inwards and up the bat – up from the point at which the man at bat wishes to make contact, meaning that he is likely instead to catch it on the top edge.

Some pundits say that the reason that .300 is now so difficult to hit in professional baseball is because of sliders, one of the most difficult pitches to throw, combining for the pitcher the best of both worlds, spin and speed, and for the batter the worst.

Slow Curve is essentially a curve ball thrown more slowly, and like all slow pitching in pro baseball requires considerable deception from the pitcher. It is a change of pace pitch, one that forces the batter's swing out of synchronization with the expected speed of the ball.

A Change Up pitch is one that appears to be faster than it is, and depends on the arm action matching that for a fast ball, the slowness being created either by dragging the foot or by holding on to the ball longer than usual. Successful change up pitchers are rare and a number of great pitchers have abandoned the ploy at a certain point in their career. It is hard to deceive the batter by the basic movement in the pitch, and a change up pitch to a batter who sees it coming is like a gift of manna.

Screwballs are thrown with the spin going the opposite way to a curve. The spin makes the ball break down and away from a left-handed batter when the pitch is coming from a right-

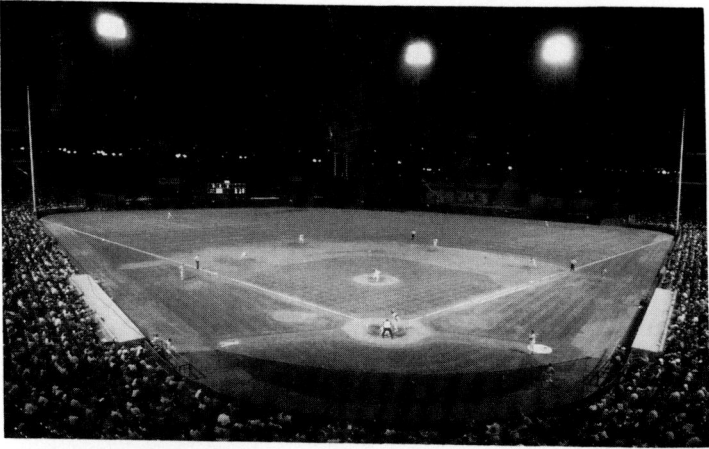

Like cricket grounds, baseball stadia vary greatly in character, and also in the shape and size of their boundary lines. Baseball played in the ultra modern Houston astrodome, and on astroturf, feels very different to baseball played in the smaller, older grass based parks like Fenway, home of the Boston Red Sox.

Above is Anaheim Stadium, home of the California Angels. Below are some of the varying shapes of baseball grounds, in some cases determined by old street patterns.   *All-Sport/Mike Harding*

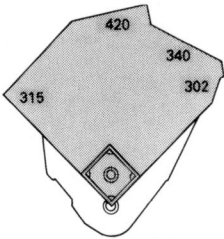

Boston Red Sox
Fenway Park
Seats 33,538

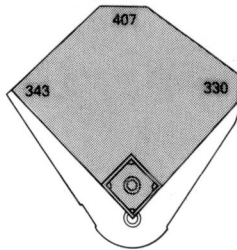

Minnesota Twins
Metropolitan Stadium
Seats 45, 919

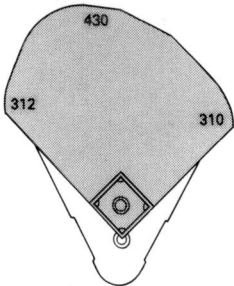

New York Yankees
Yankee Stadium
Seats 57, 545

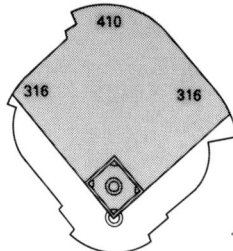

Seattle Mariners
The Kingdome
Seats 59,438

The official distance between the pitcher's plate and home plate is sixty feet, six inches. The ball travels at over 80mph and sometimes as fast as 100mph. The white block in the centre circle is the pitcher's plate and the pitcher's foot must be on this when he delivers. Just in front of the catcher (wearing 15) is the home plate. Professional hitters consider there is about one tenth of a second in which to decide whether to hit or leave the pitch as the ball travels towards them.

All-Sport

Baseball's critics argue that it is a slow game and, taken on runs scored per hour, or even hits per hour, that is true. Baseball can be slow if you only look at the hitter. But watch the pitcher and see how his fortunes change delivery by delivery and you will find it a fast game with an ever varying rhythm.   *All-Sport/Mike Powell*

Pitchers are an odd breed of individual, often more pitcher than individual, working to the ultimate of physical strength and mental concentration. Because a baseball is so hard to hit, and because the man with the bat has so few chances, it is part of the character of baseball that the pitcher is dominant. It has been described as a game designed to stop things happening!   *All-Sport/John Hayt*

Gary Carter of the New York Mets (above) and Greg Brock of the
Los Angeles Dodgers (below) attempt to hit a home run – one hit
right out of the ground in fair territory, like a six in cricket. Home
runs come seldom, and a batting average of one hit that lands the
batter on the base for every three times at bat is considered very
good indeed.   *All-Sport/Duomo, All-Sport/John Hayt*

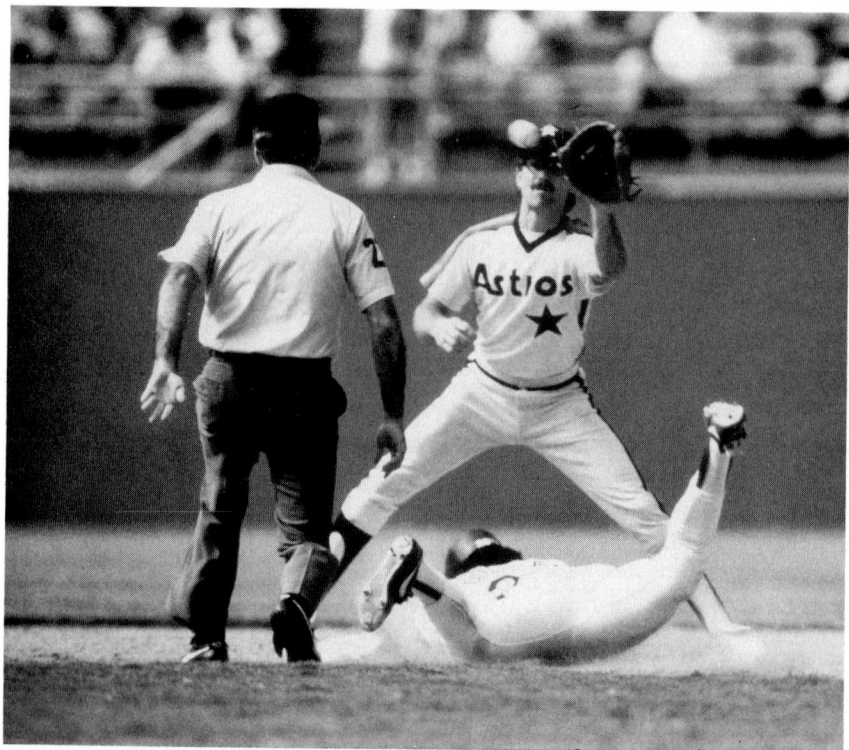

To avoid being out in baseball the man at the bat must not be caught and can only miss two straight pitches or 'strikes'. On the third he must hit and put his body in contact with at least first base before the first baseman is also in contact with both the ball and the base. This leads to some spectacular running and fielding. Here the man on the ground is diving for the base as the ball comes to the fielder's hand a split second later. *All-Sport/Mike Powell*

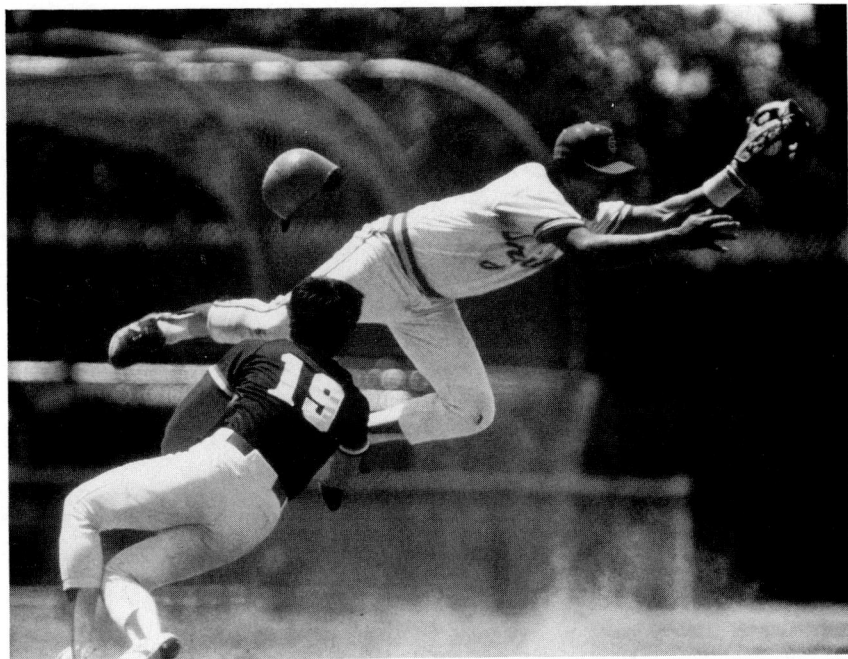

Catches made by professional baseball players often appear simple on television. They are not. They require agility (and often courage) and they depend to a great extent on positioning by the fielder and his ability to judge where the particular hitter is likely to hit the ball. Differences in fielding positions are not as extreme as in cricket but the fielders do make important, if subtle, changes. It is considered by some that positioning is as important as anything in winning at baseball. *All-Sport/A Chung*

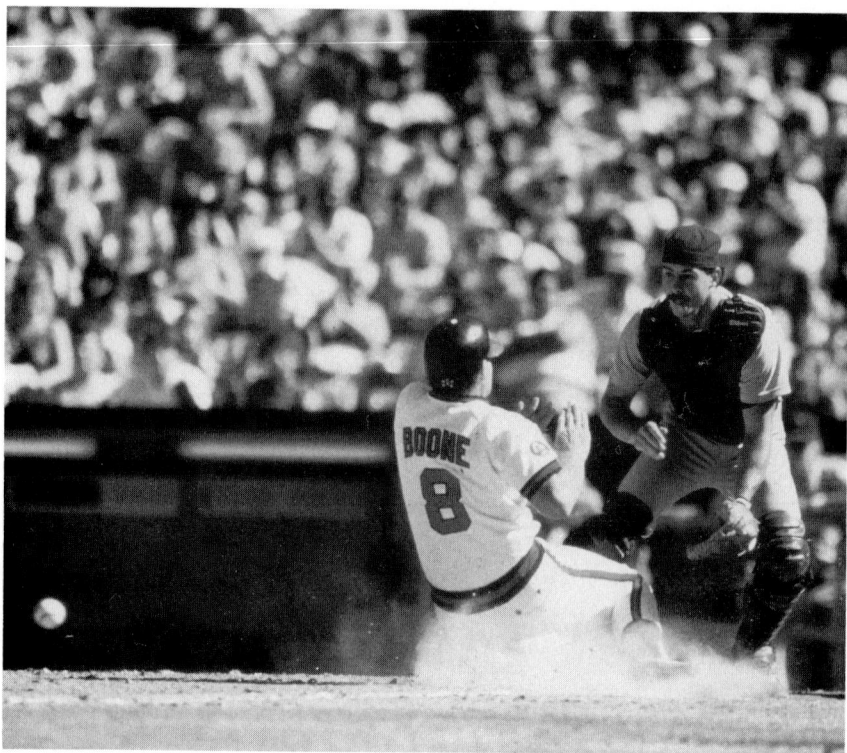

The climactic moment in baseball. The runner, number 8, plunged feet first for the home plate. The catcher, armour plated and menacing as he looks, does not yet have the ball in his hand. A run is thereby scored. *All-Sport/John Hayt*

handed pitcher. In other words this is an outward breaking pitch.

A Forkball is held between the first and middle fingers and is difficult for any but those with the largest hands. The advantage of this distorted action is that the spin which is normally created when the ball leaves the middle finger is reduced, and the ball is therefore likely to break downwards.

There are others, in particular **Knuckle Balls**, which are something of a hybrid. They are essentially balls with an odd grip, either with the knuckle, or with the ends of the fingers, or fingernails; they are slow and react more to air currents than any particular spin. Only very few pitchers have mastered them but they are useful because they are unorthodox. Thus they can be used occasionally to throw a hitter off kilter and they may be over the plate. But all too often knuckleballs end up as balls, not strikes.

The rules require the pitcher to take up two positions before pitching: The 'windup' position, is more leisurely and is used when there are no runners on base, and the 'set' or 'stretch' position, used when there is a runner. (Or, that is generally the case.) In the windup position the pitcher goes through the stretching motion while his foot is on the rubber. In the set position he does this before he puts his foot on the plate, allowing himself essentially a quicker delivery or the ability to quickly throw to a baseman if a runner is threatening to steal. At any time he may disengage from the plate, for example if he is not quite sure of the catcher's signal, but having done so he must not 'step quickly on to the rubber and pitch. This may be judged a quick pitch by the umpire' says rule 8.01 and adds: 'when the pitcher disengages from the rubber, he must drop his hands to his sides.'

It needs considerable practice to follow, particularly on television, the type and direction of pitches – rather in fact like becoming good at bird watching. A skilful ornithologist can identify a distant bird which a non-expert can hardly see. What really happens is that the expert eliminates most of the possibilities instantaneously. Something in the flight tells him that it is a hawk. There are less than ten British hawks. The approximate size eliminates most of them. The environment pins down the rest. So he can immediately say it is a marsh harrier, or a kestrel, or an eagle. Unlike an uninitiate, he does not need to consult a bird book.

The same is true of pitches and pitchers. You know that a certain pitcher never throws a certain kind of delivery. You watch his body as much as the actual ball and you watch the man at bat's reaction. You know the statistics and past performances and so you recognize the pitch for what it is.

What you can see with some ease is variation, although even this is difficult on television where the camera is often not focussing on the pitcher at all. But watching a live game you can get a sense of pace and how and how often it changes, and to what effect.

In the 'twenties and 'thirties many more pitchers would go the whole game, sometimes even pitching two back-to-back in a 'double header'. Now that is not so common and pitchers are generally relieved between the fourth and seventh inning. Seldom will a manager relieve a pitcher earlier than the fourth, even if he is being hit around, although sometimes the pitcher may tell him in consultation that he is not on form. But equally pitchers seldom go more than six innings even when they are on form. Shut-outs (where no run is scored against a pitcher) are rare. They are made even rarer by the habit of managers of changing the pitcher when he may be getting to a point where tiredness might lead to a mistake.

A result of this tactic of changing pitchers even when they are pitching well is that, over the last forty years, two breeds of pitcher have emerged, starters and relievers. Starters tend to have more stamina, their task being to hold down the opposition with consistency over the first five to seven innings. Relievers have the ability to come from behind and deal with losing situations, but they tend to have more short term and less long term energy. Thus it is not uncommon, in a bad situation, the starting pitcher having been relieved, to see things to go from bad to worse under the relief pitcher, who will then be relieved by another. Equally a relief pitcher may change the character of the game entirely. The batting order of the side to which the new pitcher belongs may have been nervous with the former pitcher, but then settles down and the runs begin to come. Pitchers do more than throw the ball and try to get the other side out. If they are clever they impose character on a game and that does a lot for their own side.

Exactly what the difference in temperament is between starters and relievers no one has defined, for some relievers, like Jim Brosnan, are laid back, phlegmatic, very much the new breed of more literate pitchers who have crept into baseball and taken over from the very taut (in personality), slightly humourless pitchers who seemed to dominate the game until the 'fifties. The new breed are men like Brosnan, or the truculent Bob Stanley, the Boston reliever. For all that, Clemens seems to be a straight-up pitcher, a personality who seems more pitcher than person, who lives and dreams pitching, body and soul put into ejecting the round object over the five-sided object at a certain specified height and speed.

Baseball is in general a game that does not require great physical fitness. Pitchers in particular will tend to drink to relieve the strain. The number chewing tobacco is less now than it was, but the chewing habit is very much of the pitcher's way of life. Any aid to concentration is worth pursuing in an activity that so much requires it.

The question of fitness is related to the question of size. Pitchers and hitters alike tend to be sceptical of too much muscle training, feeling that timing, the lucidity of the movement, can be affected by over-muscularity. There are still slight pitchers, but they are becoming the exception. The 'Complete Handbook of Baseball' for 1983 shows that among twenty pitchers who 'worked the mound' for Cleveland only one was less than six ft. one. There was one of six ft. six, two of six ft. four and a handful at six ft. three. For Kansas City in the same year the two shortest pitchers were six foot.

So the era of the big pitcher seems to be upon us, but the era of the fast-ball-only pitcher does not. There was a time when it seemed that pitching might get faster and faster, and there are pitchers who, having tried variation, settle for their fast-ball, using it to sole and devastating effect. But variation is still the hallmark of most great pitching, and is likely to remain that way.

Some things have changed. There has been a downward tendency in batting averages over the years, although more recently a rise. But basically baseball remains remarkably consistent. In athletics you can almost predict that running times in all events will be faster in ten years. In baseball it is quite likely that pitchers ten years hence will not hit the heights achieved by today's group. More than hitters, pitchers tend to come and go, reaching great heights for a short time and then settling into the middle ground. A few pitchers go on doing well season after season. But the major league statistics over the years reveal that the career of most pitchers is up and down. Clemens, for example, has had an astonishing start to his career. It is possible that next year he will be off form and the year after on. It is equally possible that he will never regain these heights. No one can tell, but unless there is unison between the pitcher's body and mind, the pitching may be good, but it will not be spectacular. Good hitters are far from two a penny, but can be found. Good pitchers are more rare, and great ones rarer still.

The character of balls does seem to have changed somewhat. The basic weight and circumference have been the same since 1892, but it is thought by some that balls in the 1930s were livelier than those of today. Certainly batting averages throughout the leagues have fallen since the New York Giants batted the record average of .318 in 1930. In recent years leading teams are lucky if they reach an average of .275, and a good number will be below that. How much this has to do with balls and how much with the quality of pitching is questionable. I am inclined to favour the latter.

The best measure of a pitcher's ability is his earned run average, or ERA, described in the glossary. Other methods of judging a pitcher's success are to compare wins and losses, or to note the number of saves, the only difficulty being that a pitcher alone does not win a game. He may have an ERA of one, but if his own side scores less than this, he is debited with a loss.

They are an odd bunch, attackers and personalities delivered to a single task. For even in the National League no one really cares how a pitcher hits. If he is a useful pitcher, that is what matters to the management, regardless of whether he seems to have eyes in the back of his head when actually at the plate.

10

MORE ON FIELDING

Statistics, like the best kind of art history, are not basically an attendant or peripheral activity. They are the means by which the act becomes articulate.
Canadian baseball fan and art historian,
                                                    Adam Gopnik

Len Tucker is perhaps the most academically minded person I know who has also played professional baseball. He is now the director of the Massachusetts Historical Society, an austere Boston institution guarding over the austere documents of the puritans and other early settlers. He wanted to be a ball player, however, and he was clearly very good indeed, as a player in minor leagues in North Carolina before World War II, and thereafter as player-manager of a team in – of all places – the Alaska League.

Because he did not quite make it, and because he is objective he knows how very, very difficult it is to reach the top. You can practice hitting and pitching and catching every day from the age of ten onwards and make your way first up the junior leagues, then into the minors, even to the AAA (triple A) minor league, essentially the second division of baseball, but never quite have the extra to make the top.

The minors are where a lot of players stick, and Len Tucker was one of them. But when he talks about baseball, which he does lyrically, he keeps coming back to the subject of fielding. I think the term 'chess on grass' has been coined by others, but it was Len who made me see – or begin to see – what was at issue, and what is least visible to all but highly experienced fans, namely that there is a great deal more to fielding tactics and strategy than meets the eye. The term is 'setting up the play'. The fielding side is continuously setting up plays for the man at bat, working with the pitcher to force him into a particular situation. Equally the batting side, especially when there are men on bases, is setting up plays to deceive or defeat the field.

Here is an example. There are runners on first and third, a potentially dangerous situation. The pitcher encourages the steal by throwing a ball. The catcher then encourages the man on third to run home by throwing to second, but the second baseman immediately throws it back to the catcher so that the man running from third is out. Thus second base is allowed to be stolen, but the man on third, the dangerous and potentially scoring man is out.

This is called a 'delayed double steal'. A 'hit and run' is, in a sense, the opposite. A runner on first keeps niggling the pitcher by attempting to steal. He thereby forces the second baseman back to second base rather than to the first base side of second base, his normal defensive position. A gap has then opened between first and second base and, if the man at bat handles it right he hits through this gap, but well short of the outfield, so that the stealer may even get to third while the man at bat gets to first, thereby creating a very dangerous situation. It is different from a straight steal, and riskier, for to get round, the runner starting at first has to go like hell the moment that the pitcher's delivery begins. And this, if it does not work, can well result in a double play, with two men being run out.

But it does show the intensity of tactics, how both sides continuously strive to pin each other down.

In all this the key really lies with first and second base and the short stop, who have a great deal of infield to defend and need to be in the right relation to each other – and the bases – to make the outs when runs are attempted. In Pete Rose's view, second base is the most difficult place to play. In the view of many others it is short stop. Third base is difficult to play as well but statistics suggest that it produces fewer tricky plays, because there are more often runners to or at first and second. There is an argument that the tedium and the small amount of room for manoeuvre do make third base the more difficult position. There is validity to all these opinions but Rose's view is given extra clout when he says that 'the most important play in baseball is the double play' and 'the most important man in the double play is the second baseman'. The point is that in most double plays the second baseman is the pivot. It is he who has to predict the play, make sure he is guarding the gap between first and second and then make the catch at second, keep his foot on the base, pivot round to first with the runner coming straight at him, and make a very fast and sure throw to first, sure because the first baseman must have his foot on the bag at the time he recieves the ball in order to make the out.

One way to appreciate fielding is to sit in the bleachers, the seats on the far side of the park. They are the least expensive, though rowdiest seats in the ground, but from them you can concentrate on the field. The problem with sitting in the bleachers is that they are far away, but being behind the field you get a fielder's perspective rather than the hitter's/pitcher's perspective which most of the seats along the right and left foul lines give you. And you may be rewarded by seeing a great outfield catch close to, something the rest of the spectators are denied.

One thing to notice is that fielders have definite character-istics, even physical characteristics. Short stops are generally small and agile, and second basemen usually the same. First basemen tend to be tall, and are often big hitters without the big throw that is needed for the outfield.

Tall men are selected for first base because they can reach for the ball without having to leave the bag in a close situation. Many of them are left-handers – that is left-handed for throwing, right for catching – because most of their throws, to second and third are to their right. But there are many right-handed first basemen. The big problem for first and second basemen is that they have to defend the bases, first and second being the most commonly run to and from. But they also have to defend the gap between them, against pulled shots by left-handers or driven shots by right-handers.

Infielders, particularly short stops and second basemen, may be chosen for their ability as fielders, with their hitting ability considered secondary. Great short stops are hard to find, rather like great goal-keepers. Being the people who stop very hard hits going to the outfield, they can make or break games and their agility is legendary, so much so that there was once a ballet written about a short stop. The outfield tends to go to men with strong arms. With the boundary a minimum of three hundred feet from home plate, an outfielder who can reach the catcher with a single throw of up to a hundred yards may be able to prevent the most crucial man on base, the man at third, from reaching home plate. Outfielders are generally, but not always, the big hitters on the team, and there is no doubt that playing the outfield is not as tricky as playing the infield.

Finally there is the catcher, a man whose role is far more important than just catching well. Catchers take continuous punishment and in spite of additional padding to their gloves often suffer badly from bruised and damaged hands. They call many of the pitches, that is directing them by a series of signals to the pitcher, using a short hand of signals which they must be careful to disguise from the third base coach on the batting side, last he transmits them either to runners or to the man at bat. They often set up deliberate walks, and in bunting situations the way they move to the ball is often crucial. They often get hit by the ball when it tips the bat and strikes foul backwards. They have to be most alert when things go most wrong, that is when a pitcher throws a pitch that is way off kilter and failing to catch the ball clean, they have to turn and gather it up, discarding mask and hat and trying to lumber around in heavy chest armour and leg guards. Officially there are no captains in baseball but the catcher is generally the *de facto* boss.

In stature catchers are usually short and stocky. In temperament they are almost always buoyant characters. It has been said that becoming a catcher is the easiest way into the majors, because not many people want the unglamorous job of being punished by balls all the time, during hours of crouching near the sand. That may be, but you seldom see a bad catcher, and when you have a good one he does an incalculable amount to bring a team together in difficult situations, and to control the pitcher. One way he does this is to control the pace of the game. Pitchers can dally and hitters can dally too, and ask for time out before the pitcher has wound up, a way of upsetting his rhythm and a device sometimes allowed by umpires, who tend to give rather than deny time out. But catchers, by the way they hold on to the ball for a time or return it briskly, can do a lot to help niggle a batter. They are also frequently abusive, not when the pitcher is winding up, but with cynical remarks as the batter reaches the plate. One catcher, for example, always used to ask certain men coming to bat: 'How's the family?' It infuriated them, they dreaded it, but it was not against the rules.

Chess on grass is a useful concept in several ways. It describes the intensity of positioning when little movement (or none) may be visible. And it suggests – unless you are a very great expert at chess – that more is happening than meets the eye. To appreciate it, either sit behind the game, as suggested above, or watch only a few fielders, difficult of

98

course on television where others select your view. But if you get the chance, watch for example just how varied the positioning of the third baseman is throughout the game – not much in physical terms, ten feet in when he suspects a bunt, ten feet back when he is against a big hitter, tight on the base when there is a runner, loose when there is not, to the left of the base against a right hander who has difficulty pulling pitches. It is a study in detail, and a rewarding one.

◇ 11 ◇

A NOTE ON THE UMPIRES

Umpires got to be stupid to begin with or they wouldn't take the job.

Attributed to a professional manager

Overabused and underpaid, at least in relation to major league players, umpires in baseball have a task which, to most outsiders, is thankless. They have little home life in the season. They stand out in the sun concentrating for more accumulated hours than any player. They are abused by pitchers, catchers, fielders, batters, managers, coaches and crowds. They are seldom noticed except when they make a mistake, and when the video reveals that they have made a mistake, audiences and television and radio commentators revel in the matter.

There are four umpires in the game, one at each base. They wear a standard uniform provided by the League, consisting of grey slacks, light blue shirt, navy blue blazer and blue baseball cap. The plate umpire has to wear a face mask, throat protector, chest protector and shinguards under his trousers.

Before the game begins the umpires are provided by the home team manager with thirty new balls in packages of six, sealed and bearing the name of the League President. The umpires are then charged with rubbing mud into them to take off the sheen. Until 1938 they made a mud pie from any old dirt lying around, but in that year the Philadelphia coach, Lena Blackburn, dissatisfied with the scratches this created, went in search of something better and came up with a goo based on fine sand, which he began to sell in tins. He said it came from the Delaware river, but pundits suspect it hails from a less romantic location in New Jersey. For all that the substance from the Lena Blackburn Rubbing Mud Company is now what the umpires have to use, at a cost of about fifteen dollars or ten pounds a tin.

The umpires are charged with other pre-game duties. They have to police the ground to see that there is no fraternization between the two sides, a rule which they find embarrassing and which the players find absurd, the argument being that if there was to be any hanky panky it could be done on the 'phone or outside the ground, and that the players know each other anyway, having played with each other before, having met regularly on the League circuit. Still the commissioners insist. The World Series of 1919, fixed with bookies by Chicago players, has not been forgotten.

The umpires also have to go over ground rules, which are local rules governing, for example, what exactly makes a home run. Another might deal with balls that bounce out of the game from fair territory, which usually merit an automatic two base hit. They have to check the lights, the dimensions and markings of the pitch, and the bats, which must be made to an exact standard.

With the game ready to begin, the third base umpire delivers a dozen balls to the plate umpire, who keeps them in small bags attached to his belt. This and all the rest of the padding and things carried in blazer pockets tend to make plate umpires look a bit like Humpty Dumpty. The rest of the balls go to the ball-boy, who keeps the umpire replenished as the game goes on.

Over the season umpires rotate from base to base, but during any one game the plate umpire has the most concentrated work. Because the strike zone varies, depending on the height and crouch of the player at bat, he has to be adept at visualizing the invisible rectangle above the plate which is the strike zone, defined by the corners of the plate and the area between the armpits and knees of the man at bat. Thus the umpire must adapt his own stance or crouch to get the best view of each man at bat. It is a considerable skill because he has to think in three dimensions, not only horizontally and vertically, but also at a distance from himself, since a ball heading for the plate at one point may, a foot further forward in its flight, break just to the right or left of the plate. If it is difficult in tennis for the umpires to see the line exactly, this is that much more difficult.

Exactly where the home plate umpire stands depends on complicated rules set up by the two Leagues. In the National League he stands almost level with the catcher, and views pitches between the catcher's left shoulder and the batter's right shoulder, assuming a right handed batter. In the American League he stands in a position which looks more comfortable for all concerned, just behind the catcher, but with the risk that the catcher may obscure his view.

The home plate umpire is responsible for calling balls and strikes. For this he usually carries a ball and strike indicator, a small tallying device. He also carries a whisk-broom, a small brush for cleaning sand off the plate, and a pad on which to note changes in the line-up, the introduction of pinch hitters and so forth. He also has to decide on balks by the pitcher – when the pitcher breaks his action and fails to pitch. He and the others also watch for pitchers putting spit or other substance on the ball, for rule 3.02 states 'no player shall intentionally discolour or damage the ball by rubbing it with soil, rosin, paraffin, licorice, sand-paper, emery paper or any other foreign substance', the point being that foreign substances including spit can affect the pitcher's grip on the ball, and hence its flight.

Pitchers are continuously niggling umpires by moving their hands across their lips, taking off or tweaking their caps, etcetera, before making their wind-up, and there are undoubtedly ways of getting spit onto the ball undetected. For all that umpires seldom catch pitchers tampering with the ball.

Umpires can be abused for both the calls they make and for their decisions on runs. They get sworn at for calls, but the rules give them an inviolable position. Once they call a ball or strike, there is no appeal. More controversial are the calls they make on balks (or fail to make, for a balk is very difficult to define) and on runs scored or bases reached. Managers in particular will come right out, stand an inch away and start yelling at them, something which not infrequently leads to the expulsion of the manager from the game, or even to his suspension. Some managers are notable for such behaviour, especially Yogi Berra, the now deposed Yankee manager. Whenever I saw a Yankee game and he was managing, out he would come. And of course the crowd loved it. Ralph Houk, one of the most successful managers in modern baseball, has frequently been ejected.

The umpires at the three bases get abused less often, partly because they make fewer decisions. Although they seem to stand still for much of the game, there is a great deal of skill in umpiring at the bases, because they must place themselves in a position to see both the base, and whether the ball has been caught.

Among the most difficult calls for an umpire to make are:

Double Plays. Say there is a runner at first and the ball is hit to the second baseman. He will attempt to run out the runner moving to second, and then throw to first so that the batter can be thrown out as well. If he has to move in to second base at the time of making the play, he must have the ball in his hand when his foot is on the bag. This requires extremely close judgement by the umpire, for the baseman will throw the ball as soon as he can and that may be before his foot is on the base. If this happens the run to second has to be allowed even if the other man reaches first.

Half Swings. The man at bat must check his swing if he decides he is facing a ball, and not a pitch into the strike zone. This is difficult to call because some movement forward by the bat is both legal and inevitable. If the umpire decides that a swing has been made, then it counts as a strike against the batter, even though the ball was wide of the plate. Officially a swing is considered to be so once a player 'breaks' his wrist backwards, but it is difficult for the plate umpires to see half swings, because they are so close to his eyes which are focussed on the strike zone. So third base umpires often call them, or plate umpires defer to third base umpires on the call.

Foul Pop-ups. From time to time the ball catches the top edge of the bat and goes almost vertically up, sometimes into foul territory. There is not much room here behind the plate, and the umpire has to watch the ball for the catch while getting out of the fast-moving catcher's way – and out of the way of the catcher's mask, as it is flung aside. In reality this is not so much a difficult call to make as a difficult call to make way for, with umpire and catcher from time to time getting tangled in each other, with the result that the umpire has to rule umpire's interference. Another difficult call for an umpire, one that requires a good deal of subjective judgement, is running off the baseline by a runner, subjective judgement because there is no visible measure of the distance allowed and also because rule 6.05(k) makes exception for runners getting around fielders.

Gradually the status of umpires has improved. In the early days baseball was corrupt and rough in the extreme. Grounds were badly managed and crowds would often break onto the field and abuse the umpires. In one case an umpire was even attacked with an ice pick. Today the abuse is gentler. The San Diego Padres have a mascot which parades around before the game, a man dressed up as a chicken, a bit like a giant Muppet show character. Part of his routine is to eat a dummy umpire, but that is about as violent towards umpires as fans get.

Ever since the fixed World Series, and the consequent introduction of commissioners as police of both Leagues, the status of umpires has been improving. In the 1920s Bill Kelm was an umpire who introduced a much tougher attitude – and a more courageous one – among umpires. Considered among the greatest in the history of the game, it was he who announced 'I never made a wrong call in my life', something umpires still remember to say to themselves in intimidating situations. Kelm invented the signs still used by umpires:

- a right hand extended, for a player out.
- both arms raised, for when the ball is dead.
- a signal like a policeman beckoning traffic forward, to carry on the game.
- a signal like a policeman stopping traffic, when time out is called by a batter and the pitcher must wait.
- the right hand raised high, for an infield fly.
- both hands swept sideways, to show that a runner is safe at a base.

Kelm and another umpire of this period, Tom Connolly, an Englishman with an Irish name, did a lot to improve the standards of the game between the wars, and have been rewarded with places in the Hall of Fame.

Financial status took longer in coming. But in 1968 the Major League Umpires Association was formed. Umpires struck in 1970 and 1979, the press got merry with all kinds of jokes about calling strike, and the umpires were unpopular with everyone; but from having been miserably paid they now make up to seventy thousand dollars a year, with a bonus for the World Series, and with their cumbersome gear carted around at the League's expense.

Umpires vary in temperament, evinced in the way they make their signals, particularly where they call 'strike' and signal with the right hand. In the minor leagues, and sometimes for the benefit of television audiences, they do this flamboyantly, as if relishing in the process. But the wiser and more experienced know that such display hides a basic inner weakness, that when it comes to the difficult calls they have to behave truthfully, and that when abused by players often the best course is to stop the play, bend down and wipe the plate with the small hand brush they carry, the whisk-broom, and blithely say nothing. Of such gestures is great umpiring made, and professional baseball is so tense – 'tight' is the Americanism – that continuously great umpiring is required to prevent teams getting out of hand.

It is a job that requires a very great deal of concentration. In a nine inning game the umpires between them will have to call around three hundred deliveries as balls or strikes. They will have to declare about seventy runners safe or not safe on bases. They will have to watch at every pitch for checked swings and balks. They will have to be right on all of them. They must also be intelligent and experienced in terms of placing themselves, particularly the base umpires, who need to move fast to avoid interference and to see either catches or tags being made. An umpire must never allow himself to get out of sight of the base and in, for example, a double play or a bunt situation, that can mean thinking and moving fast. They have to be deft about not getting hit by the ball – which happens about once every game, usually from foul tips when the plate umpire is the victim – but they also have to be firm in their positioning, so that they are not thrown off by the basemen.

The rules of basball are not complicated, but the interpretation of them requires considerable judgement. Standing up to major league players and managers who have a lot at stake in each call is no easy task, in spite of the fact that rule 9 gives them almost absolute power, in particular including a clause reminiscent of a rule from the most authoritarian of Victorian grammar schools: 'all rules shall be obeyed, whether written or unwritten, and any rule disobeyed shall be punished by caning'. The baseball equivalent is 'each umpire has the authority to rule on any point not specifically covered in these rules' and this is backed by the all-encompassing 9(D) which says 'each umpire has authority to disqualify any player, coach, manager or substitute for objecting to decisions'. It goes on to say that anyone can be ejected from the game for bad language, and for arguing with the umpire.

Were players and coaches mute, it would be easy. The reality is that they are not, and that for all the strength of the rules they do argue with acrimony in tight situations. They also try to cheat.

Interference with the ball by pitchers has already been mentioned; there was a case where a pitcher for Seattle, Rick Honeycutt, was caught with a thumb tack under a bandage on his hand, suitable for nicking the skin of the ball. Sharpening the eyelets on the pitcher's glove is another trick. Bats are also played around with, generally to add weight to the bottom end. Mercury is said to have been used for this, and Graig Nettles of the Yankees once broke his bat when hitting and out came a whole lot of those exceptionally bouncy rubber balls that children play with. Base coaches may help runners to the base when they think the umpire is not looking, and runners will often run wide. Fielders will also jump around to disturb a batter's concentration. An estimate, made by one professional baseball writer, that fifty percent of all pitchers put something on the ball, may be high. But it illustrates that umpires are involved in a continuous game of cat and mouse.

Umpires need size, both in terms of character and physique. Emotionally they must never allow themselves to feel guilty if they fear they have made a wrong call. Physically they may need to keep big men apart, and most umpires are themselves over six feet tall. They are an odd breed, for some reason tending to be overweight, perhaps because they have no one else but themselves to talk to as they circle the country, staying in hotels strictly segregated from players and managers. Perhaps it is because most players, with the exception of some big hitters and some pitchers, tend to be lithe and trim. By contrast umpires always seem to bulge, their coats never quite big enough to contain their figures. For all that they can and do intimidate managers and best players alike. And that deserves respect. Good baseball depends on them and they, to a significant extent, create it.

◇ 12 ◇

ON PARKS REGULAR
AND IRREGULAR

Fine drops of rain
run down like young streams from
plastic summer parkas
down the arms of curved chairs
falling from the hair of
three men in row 38B . . .
from Sandra Soto Hatfield's poem *Riverfront*, about
rain in the ballpark.

Before the World Series of 1986 when the New York Mets
came to play the Boston Red Sox in a charity exhibition game
in the early autumn, they gasped. Down on the field they saw
something they had heard about but never seen, the famed
Boston 'wall', the huge left field fence that has been there
since early Fenway Park days to protect passers by on Lands-
downe Street. It was very different, this cliff of green, from
anything in the Mets' own ground, the more modern Shea
Stadium, out in the Long Island suburbs beyond La Guardia
airport.

Apart from the fact that there is astroturf in some National
League grounds, the dimensions on a baseball field are strictly
and officially regulated, with this exception: the boundary
lines differ.

109

Some people in baseball revile this. It is impossible, they argue, to compare like with like if a major ingredient of the equation is irregular. For example, they argue that Babe Ruth's home run hitting record with the Yankee teams of the 1920s would never have been so high had he stayed with the Red Sox. True, Yankee stadium has among the shortest right and left field boundary lines, only three hundred and twelve and three hundred and ten feet, and the boundary fence is low. The left field wall at Fenway is three hundred and fifteen feet from the plate, and high, so a left field homer at Yankee Stadium may not (depending on how high it is hit) be a left field homer at Fenway. And Ruth hit a lot of left field homers. Given that the fascination of statistics is not just as a guide to what happened but also as a stimulus to asking what might have happened, the possibilities are endless. What if Ruth had stayed at Fenway?

The statistics at this point become complicated. Ruth played only half his games at home anyway, and anyway a lot of his Yankee Stadium homers went well beyond the boundary line. It is true that Detroit players have a particularly tough time because the furthest out point on the boundary is four hundred and forty feet, ten feet further away than on any other ground. The ground with next longest boundary, four hundred and thirty feet, is Yankee Stadium, although it is notoriously small at the right and left field line. But the argument for uniformity goes round in a circle; for if you say that it would give greater statistical comparability to the game, you come up against the wall of sheer impracticability – that it is not going to happen. And the fact that the Mets marvelled at Fenway, at the challenge in that particular quarter of the field, suggests the truth about this matter of dimensions, namely that most fans glory in the eccentricity of their home ball parks, arguing that while this may prevent quantitatively comparing like exactly with like, qualitatively it adds a lot to the game, a living part of its history.

Fenway Park in Boston is, in many ways, a horrible place. It is right in the urban part of Boston and you cannot park there except at outrageous prices charged by touts with access to vacant lots. If you do manage to park, you cannot leave until everyone behind you has left, so closely crammed are the cars. The Fenway Park management always urges fans to come by public transport, but Boston public transport is worse than a bad joke, consisting of tramways and buses whose vehicles never come and routes never interconnect. The entrances to Fenway are dingy, the wooden seats barely comfortable and lacking leg room. The beer is thin and the hot dogs execrable.

But I love it and cherish it. For all the discomfort, the stadium is small. With reasonably priced seats you can feel right on top of the green carpet. It has grass. It has an eccentric boundary with a high wall and a small indentation just behind centre field, just to the left of the new electronic scoreboard which sits above the bleachers, the cheapest seats of all. A driven ball hit high landing in this indentation may have the fielder turning circles as if he were in a fives' court, but it will not score a home run; whereas five yards to the right it would. Most important, there is something immediate about Fenway Park which is lacking in the larger, more modern fields: a sense of contact with the game. And while there is plenty of reason to complain about the transport and the catering, there is a character about the place that I would not swop for all the astrodomes in the world. The attendants wear old fashioned uniforms with peaked caps surrounded by wickerwork, like bus conductors in a James Cagney movie. They seem about as old as this and they are always courteous. The experience of going up into the lit park from the dirty, cavernous underside of the stadium, grey concrete and grey green girders, a smell of urine and beer and sweat, is like going from a kind of hell into a kind of heaven. Under the lights everything is brighter than life, and beyond the stadium is the Boston skyline. If you are sitting in right field, there is the skyline to the west, old apartment blocks from the twenties against pearl and amber on a pleasant night. If you are sitting in left field, behind the third base line, you see night falling on the gaunt structure of the Prudential building, grey against grey blue. The park is old and worn and loved and urban. And there is a just sense of sobriety here, no chicken mascots, no dancing girls, just good old-fashioned baseball, the old red and green lights telling you where you are in the inning, with an equally old mechanical score board above them. But the greatest thing is the irregularity of the boundary. That adds a lot. Fenway homers into left field are great homers, and they and the place etch themselves on the memory.

The history of the irregularity of ball parks reflects the early days of baseball, when there were no boundaries in the area between the foul lines. Originally played on meadows where the diamond might be mowed or sanded, the further you could hit the ball into the next hayfield, the more chance you had of running round. It was only when baseball began to be played more professionally, and in urban areas, that the boundary line and then the boundary fence were established. With the boundary lines came the home run, the orgasm of modern baseball. These fences were partly there to protect passers by, but mainly to exploit a capitalist tendency: with a fence high enough for all but the brave to climb, the rest had to pay admission to see the game. Even so the idea of hitting the ball right over the fence did not really alter the style of the game, tactics up to then being immortalized in a phrase attributed to a coach called Wee Willy Keeler: 'hit 'em where they ain't'; hit the balls where the fielders are not. That was, and still is, the essence of good hitting. Most bases are made not on homers, but on singles and doubles, and they always depend on placing.

Indeed right up until the nineteen-twenties, the art of baseball was not so much to hit home runs, but to score by singles, by steals and by fielders errors. The home run was considered somewhat crude and balls hit high, if not hit high

112

enough, were fly balls and caught. Coaches' emphasis was on hitting ground balls.

But then two things happened, or rather one had been happening for some time. First, the standard of fielding improved, the statistics showing a steady decline in the number of stolen bases and bases reached on errors. Second, Babe Ruth showed how home runs could be hit.

On the whole modern stadia have tended to be built to smaller and more regular proportions, smaller because owners know that big scores bring big numbers of fans and that, although baseball is and always will be a pitcher's game, fans love to see balls hit. So do I, but baseball is as much about unrequited love as requited. The proportions are more regular because stadia can be built on virgin ground in the suburbs or beyond, with vast car parks around them, so modern architects, who love standardization, build standardized ball parks. The Houston Astrodome is three hundred and forty feet to both left and right field, and the boundary line traces almost exactly the radius of a circle whose centre point is at home plate. Riverfront Stadium in Cincinnati is almost the same, but three hundred and thirty feet to the right and left boundary lines, and four hundred and four feet to the farthest point, two feet less than in Houston.

Talk to any baseball fan and you will find that the pleasure of baseball, as of all great competitive sports, lies as much in comparing the past with the present as in enjoying the latter. That is another reason why the relatively modern Mets took such delight in visiting and playing at Fenway – which they would normally never do unless they met Boston in the World Series. When you go to Fenway, you are stepping back into the past. You can trace the way the old ground has been developed. Because it is small, holding only thirty-three thousand five hundred people as opposed to Veterans' Stadium in Philadelphia, which holds sixty thousand five hundred, and most of the other modern stadia which hold over fifty thousand, there is a particular sense of intimacy. At Shea

Stadium in New York you can be in moderately expensive seats, but feel some way from the play, with behind you tiers of concrete reaching skyward. At Fenway any decent seat gives you the feeling that you are in contact with the players.

But it is not just Fenway that is different. Talk to Los Angeles or Chicago fans, to those from Cincinnati or Houston, old or new they feel a special affinity for the ground where their team plays. They will despise astroturf or they will like it for the livelier effect it has on ground balls, for the extra difficulty it gives to bunting, for the glitter of the scoreboard and the hoopla of mascots and dancing girls in which some teams indulge, but others consider immodest. A recent nostalgic book about stadia old and new has as its title *Green Cathedrals*. In a game millions worship, their place of worship is important.

◇ 13 ◇

WHERE IT CAME FROM

For hundreds of miles around, black night, the lamps
of Desolation are lit to a childish sport, but the Void is
a child too – and here's how the game goes:. . . .
                    Jack Kerouack, *Desolation Angels*

Cooperstown, New York, is a few miles from US route 20,
which used to be the Boston post road, a main route west, but
has now been bypassed by the New York State thruway. The
post road is a little like the more famous route 66 and, as you
go lolloping straight over the hills on a dual carriageway with
little traffic, through scrubby farmland, you get a sense of
going back into the past. There is no modern glitter, no
McDonalds or pizza huts or neon, just pleasant little brick
and wood towns of which Cooperstown is one of the most
important. It has a remote, rural feeling to it, even though
only a hundred and twenty miles from Yankee Stadium.

The setting is important because it reinforces the middle
American nature of baseball, not middle American in the
derogatory sense that is applied to the lumpen, conservative
and unsophisticated vote of the middle west, but in the sense
that this is America untrammelled by imported sophisti-

115

cations; basically a farming nation, hard working, hard playing and, very often, both hard drinking and hard praying. Cooperstown seems the right place for the institution that celebrates baseball and its past, because the game began in small town, farming America. Indeed specifically it is supposed to have begun in Cooperstown.

Myth has it that sometime in the summer of 1839, Abner Doubleday laid down the rules of baseball in a game played on a Cooperstown meadow. Myth also has it that Doubleday, who became a general in the civil war, fired the first shot for the Union against the Confederate states, and that he owned the first San Francisco cable car. Bewhiskered and self-important, Doubleday during his lifetime did a lot to reinforce his self-important role in baseball. The Doubleday myth grew as the memory faded, and in 1939 the commissioners, players, owners, and managers decided to celebrate the centennial of the 'American Game' with the establishment of the Hall of Fame in Cooperstown.

If anywhere, part of New York City that is now built on, but was then open field, should house the true shrine to baseball. Modern historians doubt Doubleday's claim and tend to credit Alexander Cartwright, a New York fireman who later became a surveyor, with being the instigator of modern baseball. He, it seems, established the existing distance between the bases, introduced the three strike out rule and the three out innings. There was, however, no limit to the number of innings played and teams just went on until exhaustion or darkness overcame them. The pitcher was forty-five (not sixty and a half) feet from the plate, and only under arm pitching was allowed.

The history around Cartwright's period is difficult to sort out, the earlier history even more so. But it seems almost certain that two forms of stick and ball had been played in America since the early white settlements, one on something like a wicket, the other on something like a baseball diamond, one where you ran up and down, one where you ran round.

Because of distances and lack of modern communications various forms of the round ball game existed, town ball, stick ball and various others. Sometimes games lasted until one team had twenty runs, generally until players were exhausted. But even if Cartwright's exact contribution must be open to some doubt, the proof was, it seems, in the pudding. The version of the game he devised was tighter and it caught on. There was a logic to the limited number of strikes and the sixty feet distance between the bases, and from that is modern baseball derived. Gradually more leagues were formed, playing Cartwright's rules, and the work he had done was continued by an Englishman Henry Chadwick.

Just an aside for those who might travel to the US: the Hall of Fame consists of the Hall itself, a shrine rather like a large marbled art deco funeral parlour, with the plaques in honour of the great players arranged around the edge; a place to which American families trek thousands of miles in their chevrolets, as Romans trekked on foot and by mule to the shrines of their gods. At the side of the Hall of Fame there is a large library and a museum which combines liveliness with real detail about the game. You can know a very great deal about baseball and still learn more from the Cooperstown museum. Moreover, it is quite honest about the mythical qualities of Doubleday's claim. Cartwright is given his due and so is Henry Chadwick.

Chadwick, after his arrival in the US, lived in New York and worked as a music teacher until he became a professional baseball writer. It was he who did more than anyone to publish the rules, and the fact that he also published and wrote about the rules of cricket suggests that he had one game very much in mind when thinking about the other.

At first baseball was, like cricket, a gentleman's game, or at least very much an amateur game in which professionalism was despised. But by 1870 professionals were beginning to appear, and since then have dominated the game. College baseball is of a fair standard, but generally if one is to make

117

the major leagues he has to be scouted young and practice the game full-time from about the age of seventeen – one reason why there are so few college-educated professionals today. After about 1870 there never could have been a 'gentlemen versus players' game in which the gentlemen had much chance. The players were just too good. There is something as American about this as the converse fact that in England the gentlemen were a force in cricket right up to the 1950s.

In 1870 the under-arm pitch was still the rule, thrown with a straight arm as in under-arm cricket, and the pitcher was still forty-five feet from the plate, instead of the sixty and a half feet that he is today. Nor did the home run exist, except that players would quite often run round all the bases after a hit. By 1870 bunting had been invented. The most agile fielder would be placed at shortstop. Outfielders would shift according to whom they were playing, pitchers changed speeds, and you tried to find a left hander to play first base.

The first professional league started in the middle west in 1871, spreading east. Because the league system was informal and anyone could join, by 1876 a number of the better teams split off to form the National League, and in doing so made a move that has much to do with the character of baseball ever since. They essentially transferred the power to the owners of the teams who still have a powerful hold over their players, thus giving the game a feel that is closer to professional soccer than to cricket, the player a property to be speculated with, sold or bought. With the beginning of professionalism came the beginning of record keeping. There was no World Series as yet, and the difference in standards between teams was much greater than it is now. Nor were the home run scores high, nine being the record in 1879, but high batting averages were similar, somewhere around .400 hits per inning being very difficult to achieve.

Then in the 'eighties and 'nineties came a period of turbulence. During the 'eighties the rules changed frequently. With the owners in charge, gates became an important

118

criterion and a good deal was done to speed up the game. In 1880 a pitcher had been allowed eight balls before a walk was allowed. This number was brought down year by year, so that by 1889 it was four, as it is today. During the decade there were numerous experiments with pitching. The pitcher's box was brought back from forty-five feet to fifty. A run up was still allowed, and over-arm pitching began to come in. For a time flat bats were allowed, and the rule saying that the men at bat walked to first base if hit by the ball was established. The stolen base began to come in, and as the speed of pitching increased became somewhat common. Catchers were not yet equipped with the protection necessary for dealing with fast balls, and a number of bases were reached as wild and fast pitches eluded the catcher.

Tactics also took on a somewhat bizarre character. With money at stake for winning teams, a practice of abusing the opposition became quite commonplace, particularly shouting at the opposition pitcher to destroy his concentration. As the St Louis team did this with particular virulence, and also won games with particular consistency, other teams started to imitate the practice. From its gentlemanly origins, the ethos of baseball was becoming very different from that of cricket. Baseball was becoming a tighter and more brutal game – at least more overtly brutal. In particular coaching from the sidelines, which started with players not at bat or on bases running up and down cheering on their own runners and abusing the other sides fielders and pitcher, presaged the introduction of first and third base coaches, no longer members of the batting team. To control their activities they now have their own boxes, out of which they may not move.

There were two leagues by the early 'eighties, three by the end, the most notable being the American Association, which charged less for admission, sold beer, and was much rowdier, and the National Association, which was dry, more expensive and played a more gentlemanly – at least less riotous – game. The third league, the Union Association, was altogether a smaller affair. But while the American Association was the more raucous, it was also responsible for more of the rule changes which created today's game, many made by the St. Louis player and notorious bender of the rules, Mike 'King' Kelly, who looked not unlike Buffalo Bill. For a time a great deal of substitution was allowed, by a player 'calling himself in' to the game. Myth has it that with a potential winning hit against St. Louis that could not otherwise be caught, Kelly ran from the sidelines, called himself in and held the catch.

The mid 'eighties also saw the beginning of the World Series. It ran until the American Association collapsed in 1890, began again in 1903, shortly after the creation of the American League, but was interrupted again in 1904, when the manager of the New York Giants refused to play what he considered the upstart American League. In 1905 it resumed, and has taken place ever since.

If the 'eighties were violent, the 'nineties were more so. Immigrants were pouring into America, particularly from Ireland, southern and eastern Europe. A rural society was suddenly becoming an urban one. Professional parks were beginning to look like the parks as we know them today, and rural baseball parks, first cousins to meadows like the one at Cooperstown, were becoming anachronistic. The summers were long and hot in the cities and Irish kids could be seen playing ball on any bit of vacant ground, trooping to watch the professionals in the evenings. So virulent did things become that umpires needed police protection. Spiking of players with shoes was commonplace, runners would be held by basemen, and there were frequent fights on the ground. The results of games were also fudged for betting, particularly in Cleveland, Ohio.

The end product of this was that neither the 'eighties nor the 'nineties were attractive decades for baseball, and at times it was touch and go whether the game would really catch on. Attendances went down and violence went up. For all that, in the 'nineties the rules governing the pitcher were established.

He was set back to his present sixty feet and six inches from the plate, and he was allowed to throw with a bent arm. In 1900 he was also given the five-sided home plate, making it easier to aim for; and about this time many of the outfield fences were painted a standard dark green, making it easier for hitters to see the ball.

And so baseball entered the twentieth century. The rules have changed but not greatly. The violence has largely been curbed and women and children make up a major part of the modern audience. There have been bad moments and good, one of the worst being the fixing of the 1919 World Series by Chicago players, who were favourites, in league with Chicago bookies. It led to the appointment of a Commissioner, the head of an overseeing body with real clout. The eagle-eyed Judge Kenesaw Mountain Landis held the job from 1921 until his death in 1944, when it passed to Albert B. 'Happy' Chandler. He was voted out of office in 1950 by the owners, and there have been power struggles since, but they have never erupted so badly as to affect the state of play, being more to do with inter-league quarrels and rules governing the owners. A seven year term of office for the Commissioner has now been established.

There have been some changes in the rules. That which decreed the first two fouls should count as strikes was enacted in 1901, making things even more difficult for the man at bat. As discussed earlier, the ball has been altered. The sacrifice fly rule was abolished in 1931, then reintroduced in 1954 with the runner allowed to move only after the catch has been made. The strike zone has been through some minor changes up and down, to lower and to heighten it. And the designated hitter rule has come into the American League, still resisted by the National. There is also astroturf, but as the sentiment for the old ball parks, like Cominsky and Fenway, seems to have grown recently, it is unlikely that there will be much more of it. Essentially baseball in 1986 is not that different to baseball in 1900, at least as regards the rules that govern the game. What happens within them has been stretched from time to time. It is not an easy task; so those who stretch the potential of what can be done with stick and ball are the games' heroes.

◇ 14 ◇

ON HEROES

Appleton, who was new to the ball club, took the call, and Ruth said, 'Hey, keed, how about coming up and playing some cards with me?' He was lonesome, Appleton explained. He could not come downstairs to the lobby because he'd be mobbed by people, especially women.

From *Babe* by Robert W. Creamer

In the summer of 1984, Boston witnessed, or rather Boston fans created something called 'Yaz fever'. The career of Carl Yastremski was coming to an end. Everyone wanted to see the last moments of a phenomenon that had lasted nearly twenty years, and everyone hoped they would be extraordinary.

In reality it was a faint hope, because while Yaz had been a great player, he was by the end a solid player, still inspired occasionally, but not consistently. College educated, he had stepped into the Boston team just after another great hitter and another very great and modest hero, Ted Williams, had retired, a man who had been, perhaps, the greatest all-round hitter in baseball, an all-rounder being that rare hitter who can both hit into the midfield and choose the loose balls to clout for a homer.

Tall, slender and eagle-eyed, Williams had been the Boston hero *par excellence*. He had come to Boston at the age of

123

twenty-one and had stayed twenty-one years, winning the Triple Crown twice, the Triple Crown being awarded to one who leads the league in home runs, RBIs, and averages – a rarely given honour. In 1941 he averaged .406 and no-one has come close to this since. In 1958 he won the batting title with a .328 average, even though he was past forty. The list of honours goes on and on. Boston never won the World Series in these years, never recovered their full pre-1920 glory, but Williams and Yastremski always made it possible that they would.

Yaz' career would have been astonishing compared with anyone but Williams. He was the first player in the American League to make over three thousand hits, of which four hundred were home runs. His *annus mirabilis* was 1967 when he was twenty-eight. He too won the triple crown, with an average of .326, forty-four home runs and one hundred and twenty-one runs batted in. What fans particularly re-membered were the last few days of the season, when Boston were in the most tantalizing finish the eastern division of the American League had ever known, with four teams in the running for the pennant right through the year, continually switching place, but always within a game or two of each other.

In the final week, Boston lost two games in a row to Detroit, who were also in the top four. Boston appeared to be losing their grasp on the title, and a mood of gloom overcame the fans until Yaz came to the rescue with a batting performance in the last games and the play-offs that was still glowing in the collective memory of the team's supporters when he came to play his last games, batting in the middle of the order of a team that was a little below the middle of the eastern division.

Baseball is a sport of individuals combined in a team. There is a lot of team work, more than meets the eye, particularly in the way that fielders both co-ordinate and back each other up. A batting side needs fraternity and logic, so that the early hitters can be driven home by those in the middle, in the hot spot. But batting is a lonely activity, and pitchers are essentially loners. A team wins the World Series, but individuals make most of the copy in the record books.

Of these individuals, perhaps the greatest is Babe Ruth. He was a great player, and he was in the right place at the right time.

He was born poor. No one knows exactly when, but it was after February 1895. He was a Horatio Alger in baseball, as have been most of the greats, the college educated like Yastremski being an exception, a college player so good that he could eschew the courting of scouts until he had systematically finished his education. Solid is the word to describe Yaz; he was one of the most solid players in the history of the game. Ruth was solid too, but in a quite different way. Ruth was the son of a German immigrant bar tender in Baltimore who spent much of his time behaving as if he was in front of the bar rather than behind it. With little to keep him stable Ruth went wild on the streets, and was incarcerated for most of his youth in a Baltimore institution run by Catholic Fathers – St Mary's, a good deal closer to a Borstal than a Barnardo's. There he had the great fortune for a delinquent boy to be offered and accept discipline in something for which he had talent, pitching a baseball. Brother Matthias, prefect of discipline in the institution, was six and a half feet tall, and weighed little short of twenty stone by the time he had grown fully, the only man there bigger than Ruth, and by cudgelling and persuading he gave Ruth discipline, for which the great man was always grateful. As soon as he left St Mary's, Ruth went straight into the minors and soon to the majors. For the first time in his life he had money in his pocket.

Ruth started as a pitcher. By the age of twenty-two he was a hitter of national renown – there was something unbelievably fluid about Ruth at bat. In spite of being over seventeen stone at points in his career, he had a flexibility of swing that was unique in baseball. Big featured and big shouldered – later to be big bellied – Ruth had long spindly legs, and a way of

twisting on his hips that seemed almost double jointed. When he hit the ball, he seemed more to whip it than to crash it, and what you did not notice was how his whole body pivoted with the swing.

But it was not just that Ruth hit. He hit home runs. He broke with the tradition by which most scores were made on singles, doubles, steals and errors. In 1919 he was with Boston and hit the unheard of number of twenty-nine. Ruth was then twenty-four or less, and already a national hero. That year was the year in which corruption threatened to pull baseball apart. Ruth, by hitting big ones consistently, was re-defining the game. Ruth would hit the ball and know how he had hit it, wait a moment, watch a moment and then trot around the field on those spindly legs. He pulled crowds back into baseball, and the Ruth run became a frequently shown feature on the newsreels, a symbol of human triumph and arrogance for those who were not enjoying the benefits of the economically eclectic 'twenties. Originally he had played for Baltimore, but had been sold cynically for cash. The Boston management did likewise in 1919, when he moved to New York, nonchalant about the contractual struggles. He had already helped Boston win the World Series. With the Yankees he helped to win the American League pennant in 1921, '22, '23, '26, '27, '28 and '32, winning the World Series in '23, '27, '28 and '32. In his best years the chances were one in three that Ruth would hit a home run in the game. He averaged .342 over his career.

His appetites were enormous, for food, drink, life in the sun, women, spending money and, always, baseball. In becoming a legend he helped give baseball a legendary quality that it never achieved in its early days. He was the first baseball player to be a truly national star, alongside politicians, Hollywood faces and the seriously rich. Baseball owed him more than fine play by the time he died young, at the age of fifty-three, of an excruciating cancer of the neck, the ghost of a giant in his last days. Yes, Ruth could behave in an obtuse and arrogant way, but he came from nowhere, and to the extent that baseball can represent the conquest of life over fear, he did so.

It was not until 1961 that another hero at the plate, Roger Maris, overtook Ruth's sixty runs in a season, beating it by one. It was not until 1973 that Hank Aaron, of the Atlanta Braves, overtook Ruth's life total of seven hundred and fourteen runs.

For my money hitters make greater heroes than pitchers. Perhaps that is just because I am a normal watcher of the game. I like to see the ball hit. Or perhaps it is because baseball is such a non-game, and in making it so the pitchers are the destroyers, and the hitters the true creators. Perhaps it is because I have not played the game and so have never quite got inside pitching. Or perhaps it is because of something about the character of pitchers. There are exceptions, but often the greater the pitching they reveal to the public, the more the personality seems to distance itself. Lone rangers of the mound, they stand there, solitary and erect, with their mouths moving only around the tobacco or gum they chew, like silent outlaws in a western.

Steve Carlton, for example, was a wonder to watch, tenacious, confident and brutal. At the point at which he struck a man out for the two thousand nine hundred and thirty-third time, the left-handers' all time record, there was, according to reports from St Louis a 'wall of sound' from the fans, in spite of the fact that they were hoping for a defeat of Carlton's Philadelphia Phillies. Carlton did nothing but wait. He did not look at the crowd. He did not shake team mates' hands. He did not even touch or raise his cap. He just went on pitching – 'another day at the office', according to the report. I do not think that a hitter would ever react to a record moment like that. In Yaz' last game he was touching his cap to the crowd as often as the doorman at Claridges does to passing guests. A hitter might be flamboyant, or he might be modest, but he would not be closed to the world.

128

'Steve Carlton talks only with his arm' is how he has been captioned in a baseball book. Perhaps the best word to describe this not uncommon trait is one used by and about the Scots: 'dour'. Pitchers are very often dour men. One can see Clint Eastwood in the role: bronzed, craggy and silent.

Nolan Ryan is another modern hero of the mound, extraordinary to watch and not quite so dour as Carlton. A Texan, a cattle rancher in the off-season and a big investor, Ryan is thought to be the fastest pitcher ever to stand on the mound, the consistently fastest, a man who regularly makes the ball travel at over a hundred m.p.h. He brings a brutality to pitching that few others have shown. He is second behind Carlton in the exclusive three thousand career strikouts club (which has only has eight members over more than eighty years of history). But he is not yet in the three hundred pitching victories league, which is only marginally less exclusive with ten members, none of whom will ever come near to Cy (for Cyclone) Young's five hundred and eleven victories in the turn of the century days, before the use of relievers. Nowadays, because relievers are used so often, no-one will come near to the nearly seven and a half thousand innings that Young pitched in a career that lasted twenty years, starting in 1890 when a young man came out of the west and shattered the seasoned boards of an Ohio outfield fence against which pitchers threw in practice. As is characteristic for pitchers, he spoke by actions rather than by words. The ugly hiss of the seams in air is the pitcher's comment. Pitchers become heroes by the destruction they cause.

Besides Cy Young, the other great early pitching heroes were Christy Mathewson and Walter Johnson, who pitched for the now defunct Washington Senators for twenty-one seasons and was known as Big Train, because that was how fast his fast balls were supposed to travel. It was he who held the record for strikouts (three thousand five hundred and eight in his career) right up until the early 1980s, when Steve Carlton, Gaylord Perry and Nolan Ryan overtook him. But of all the great pitchers in the modern era, Warren Spahn must have been the greatest to watch. He was every bit the pitcher's pitcher, tall, burly, big handed, tobacco chewing, rugged faced. His career spanned the war and without his four years of service might have reached even greater heights, for pitchers often peak when they reach full strength, in their mid-twenties.

Spahn had a particularly long battle with Stan Musial, who was one of the greatest hitters of his day, and the Olympian contest between the two giants of the diamond went on for eighteen years, ending in 1963 when Musial at forty-three retired, two years before Spahn, who was then forty-four. There has never been such a hero against hero baseball battle as that between these two men.

Musial had a remarkable career average of .333, but only .314 against Spahn, although Spahn has the grace to say that Musial being a left-handed hitter, Spahn, as a left-handed pitcher should have had the advantage over him. Indeed Spahn's whole description of the contest between the two is a study in modesty and objectivity, showing just how gracious a pitcher can be off the field, while being violent on it. Musial was, says Spahn, the only hitter he would deliberately walk with the bases loaded. 'I never did discover a weakness in his batting style', he said.

Most great pitchers say nothing much beyond the mono-syllable. But Spahn had an articulate ability to analyze his game, and it helped him keep driving and driving along the sand road to the plate. It was not until he was thirty-nine that he pitched a no-hitter, in September 1960 for Milwaukee against the Philadelphia Phillies. But he did it again the next year. It remains to be seen whether Clemens or Ralph Gooden will be constantly great in this way.

Apart from stolen bases, there are five ways of measuring the greatness of a hitter's performance, the figures that must underpin a true hero. One is to do with career hits, and that record is now held by Pete Rose, who must be the best known name in baseball today – a tough, extrovert, humorous (although not always about himself) and consistent man, a real sticker who overtook the four thousand hits record of Ty Cobb that had stood since the early part of the century. For whatever is said about the increased intensity of pitching, and about the ball, whose slightly changed manufacture is said to have made it less lively in the air, there are still people who can break records. They are, and deserve to be heroes. And a remarkable number of them have been in the post-war period. There is Willie Mays, known as the 'say hey kid', the black player from Alabama who, when asked who was the greatest player of all time, voted for himself, but did so with charm and 'dazzle' – a word that has been well used about him as a performer. Mays hit three thousand two hundred and eighty-three in his career. Musial hit three thousand six hundred and thirty. 'Yaz', Yastremski, the Boston wonder boy, hit three thousand four hundred and nineteen. Altogether two have hit over four thousand, a further three – Hank Aaron, Musial and Speaker – have hit over three thousand five hundred and another nine three thousand or over, the most tragic of whom is Roberto Clemente.

Clemente came from Puerto Rico, and he hit exactly three thousand. He played for Pittsburgh and he was not a big slugger, but a steady relentless hitter of singles and doubles. He was ugly at the plate, but he had control and he had dignity, as a player and a man. He perhaps showed his control best when he hit three home runs and a double in a game against Cincinnati, driving in seven during the game. Home runs were not his thing, but he needed to show himself that he could hit them. Having done so, he went back to his normal, driving style. Shortly after this, in August 1970, he achieved a feat of ten hits in two games against Los Angeles, something no modern player has done. The first of these was partly a fluke, because it was the result of a marathon that went on for sixteen innings and until well after midnight. But the second was in a straight nine inning game, a game in the afternoon following the exhausting night before. Then on September 29th, 1972, right at the end of the season, he made his three-thousandth hit in a game against the New York Mets. Only two other living players held the record, Hank Aaron and Willie Mays. The crowd went wild at the time and the self-effacing star was abashed. Later he said: 'I give this hit to the fans of Pittsburgh and the people of Puerto Rico'. They were words that might have been corny from the lips of a lesser man.

Later that winter Clemente flew in a plane that was taking rescue supplies, which he had funded, from Puerto Rico to the victims of the Nicaraguan earthquake. The plane crashed into the sea and his body was never recovered. I learnt a lot about how important baseball is to Americans by seeing the emotion on the faces of an audience at the Baseball Hall of Fame, when a film of Clemente's life was shown.

Their ability to handle both success and failure or tragedy makes these players larger than life, and thereby baseball becomes larger than life too, a point poignantly illustrated as much by the fate of Roy Campanella as by the way people handled it.

Campanella was a stolid player who had started in the black leagues and became one of the first black players to break into the major leagues. He led the National League with one hundred and forty-two RBIs in 1953, won most-valuable player awards in 1951, '53 and '55 and was an outstanding catcher. Then, in January 1958, his car skidded on ice as he was driving home to Long Island. The thirty-six year old catcher, who had hit more home runs than any one in history, was seriously paralyzed. In his hospital room he went through a year of grim depression, refusing for much of it to have the blinds drawn, but in May 1959 he accepted an invitation to an exhibition game in Los Angeles between the two New York rivals, his own Brooklyn (soon to be Los Angeles') Dodgers, and the Yankees. He was wheeled onto the field at the beginning and made an emotional, grateful and halting speech. Then, between the fifth and the sixth innings the lights were cut, the crowd rose to its feet, and as Campanella was again wheeled onto the field, the sky was black for a moment, before everyone in the Coliseum lit a match or lighter and ninety-three thousand man-made stars appeared in the Pacific night.

You cannot have heroes without hero worship.

◇ 15 ◇

STRETCHING THE MIND

On Sunday, the breakfast process takes an extra ten
minutes, since the Averages must be consumed.
Thomas Boswell in his essay *Why time begins on
opening day*

Boswell is one of those baseball writers who argue that the
pleasure of the game comes as much in its contemplation as in
its realization, as much off the field as on. If you accept this
argument, then the standards by which you measure the
game are those set in its ultimate moments, and by the greater
players. All else is measured against what might be possible.
And what might be possible does not necessarily happen in
the final game of the World Series.

Take no hitters, for example. A no-hit, no-run game is one
in which the pitcher prevents the opposing team ever from
getting on to base – with this exception: a player can get a
walk to base either because the pitcher throws wild in a bad
patch, or because he deliberately walks a potentially strong
hitter in order to down the next man. A no-hitter happens
perhaps twice a year, and many of the best pitchers have gone
through a career without achieving one. The pleasure of

134

baseball has a lot to do with the possibility that the ultimate will happen. Perhaps it is greatest when the ultimate happens in quite unlikely circumstances.

One of the most extraordinary shutouts was by a pitcher with a chequered career. Harvey Haddix was a small, left handed pitcher who had played for a number of teams, a respectable major league player, but not among the greats. On May 29th 1959 he had a cold, and although the season was almost through its second month, he was still looking for his fourth win for Pittsburgh, the team with which he had eventually landed.

No hitters are strange games to watch because the crowd's psychology changes round. Crowds normally express emotion when their team hits, but tend to keep it to themselves when their pitcher prevents the other side hitting. But when the pitching is particularly good, the emotion switches around, and that is what happened with Haddix. He pitched with astonishing steadiness and, as every inning ended with three men dismissed, the home crowd in Pittsburgh gave him a standing ovation. The third inning went by, then the fourth, then the fifth and then the six. There were standing ovations every time by a crowd who were riveted to this unlikely man's performance.

But Haddix' own side, Pittsburgh, were also incapable of hitting the ball; or rather they were able to hit the ball from time to time – twelve hits in the course of the game – but were never able to get men right round the bases. The seventh and eighth innings went by, and then came the ninth. By the end of it Haddix had gone down in history as pitching a no hitter. Unfortunately for him the score was still tied nought-nought, and the game had to go on.

Haddix continued for two more innings. Still no hits, but still no runs by his own side. He now had pitched more no hit innings in a game than anyone in history. Then came disaster. In the eleventh inning, and deliberately, he walked the great hitter Hank Aaron. This seemed a safe tactic, but the

135

very next pitch was hit for a home run. It was the only hit against Pittsburgh that day, and it lost them the game. So tense was everyone that Aaron just ran in and failed to touch home plate. So confused was the official scorer that Aaron was given a run that was later disallowed. There had only been one hit in the game, but that was enough to lose it. Haddix' career wended on its way, but the path never took it to any other great moments of distinction.

That is what is so odd about pitchers – sometimes they get it just right, but so often the great pitchers are upset. Indeed what applied to Haddix also applied to Don Larsen, a pitcher for the Yankees in the 'fifties, who won thirty and lost forty games over four seasons in the majors, respectable but not distinguished. It was he who pitched the only 'perfect game' in a World Series, and a perfect game is even better than a no hitter, for it means that no walks are allowed. It was the fifth game of the 1956 World Series, between two New York teams, the Yankees and the Brooklyn Dodgers, a series that the Yankees won by a single game.

The opposite to this perfect game was a game of profligate, almost unimaginable scoring in which Boston hit seventeen runs in a single inning, the seventh inning against Detroit. In June 1953 the Detroit Tigers were in a badly, almost pathetically, trailing position. Of the first fifty-seven games they had won only fourteen (a record they reversed as they rolled along to the Series in 1984). At least in this particular game they managed to keep things tight until the seventh inning. Boston had scored three in the bottom of the second, Detroit had replied with two in the top of the fourth. They tied it three–three with a single in the top of the sixth, but Boston replied with another two in the bottom of that inning. It looked like a close game even when Detroit failed to score in the top of the seventh.

The Detroit pitcher in the seventh was a man called Steve Gromek, who had just joined from Cleveland. In his debut as a Detroit reliever he was bound to face some bad situations, but in this case he created one. In that seventh inning Gromeck allowed nine runs, and two other pitchers eight between them. Boston scored eleven singles, two doubles, and a home run; and six times reached bases on balls. There were no errors by fielders, so that the whole fiasco was due to the pitchers. Reports suggest Boston had a lot of luck, balls that kept just clear of infielders, or fell just short of desperate outfielders. But luck helps the lucky and Boston were on a high, never to be repeated in the majors. Ironically only some three thousand Boston fans witnessed the spectacle of their team scoring the highest number of runs in a major league inning and game. Detroit were considered that bad.

Afterwards Gromeck was in the dumps, a pitcher who was not great but who had certainly had a respectable record with Cleveland. Wondering whether he was headed for the minors, he was by his own account ignored by a stone-faced Detroit manager for several days, but then asked to pitch against Philadelphia. He did not score a shut out, but he never walked a batter and never allowed a man beyond third. Only five hits were made against him in that game, and Detroit won five–nought.

One hopes for exceptional games. Even more one hopes to see under-dogs win. You try to forget the fact, but always know that though a leading team may have beaten a trailing team in the past, there is no guarantee that the same will happen in the future.

And of course it is always most satisfying if you are backing an outsider, as Cleveland fans were in 1948. Four and a half games behind Boston in early September, the team had had a chequered year. The fans had threatened to strike when the owners tried to trade their hero and player/manager, Len Boudreau. The owners changed their mind, Boudreau stayed, the fans set attendance records, and on the last day of the season, Cleveland were tied with Boston, something which had never happened before. In order not to interfere with the play-off schedule, a game was hurriedly arranged in Boston.

Cleveland had to travel there by train, with no obvious strong pitcher, because of injuries and exhaustion. Boudreau chose a rookie, and the rookie won the game. It was an orgasmic moment for Cleveland fans, who never could have foreseen this at the time of their owner/manager crisis.

San Francisco fans were also put on tenterhooks in 1962, when against the judgement of any sane individual and any bookie, they found their team in the World Series, one in which the New York team (in this case the Yankees) behaved rather as they did in 1986 (when Mets' fans and New York newspapers speculated that Boston would not win a single game, and it went down to the seventh).

In the first game San Francisco were dispatched with authority. But they won the second. The Yankees won the third, San Francisco the fourth, the Yankees the fifth. The sixth was due to be played in San Francisco at Candlestick Park which juts into the Bay and is subject to temperamental weather. For three days it rained, but on the fourth the skies cleared and San Francisco fans watched their team come even, three–three in the series. Tension in the final game was heightened by the fact that two pitchers, Ralph Terry and Jack Stanford, were against each other for the third time in the series, each having won one so far.

The first four innings were scoreless, heightening the tension even further. In the fifth the bases were loaded against San Francisco with none out. But Stanford forced a double play and by the end of the inning the west coast team was only one down. So it went on to the eighth inning, where once again the Yankees had the bases loaded and there were no outs. Once again a double play, and the Yankees did not bring a runner home. In the bottom of the ninth San Francisco had two out, and men on second and third, when the Yankees' manager Ralph Houk came to mound. Should the pitcher walk the next man, who had scored a homer off him earlier in the season? He decided against it, and the next ball was hit like a bullet into the outfield only to be caught clean.

The Yankees took the series. San Francisco fans had been living ever since April with the impossible dream that their average team might win the series. Only in that last fifteen minutes of that October day did the dream fade. The World Series seldom fails to produce great moments. In the eight years 1955–62, six of the series went to the seventh and last game.

It is hard, seeing only excerpts on television, to appreciate just how the tension of the season develops over the American summer and fall, to get a sense of what a long road it is from spring training to the series. Once again, the best description of a baseball player's season is Jim Brosnan's book 'Pennant Race', a race won by Cincinnati for whom pitcher and writer Brosnan worked. This is not a ghosted epic, and the book deals as much with problems at airports as problems on the field. You see from the book the intense grind of a player's life, in which visits by wife and children are occasional, in which there are almost no days off, in which one hundred and sixty games are played in a season. You get a measure of the concentration required, particularly from the way that Cincinnati, a great team that year, kept falling behind, kept lapsing into losing streaks.

What players live with, supporters live with also, although in dilute form. And a lot of the drama in baseball comes from its drudgery, the long games without many hits, the way that players lapse as sides lapse. The lapse is the tunnel. At the end of it you always hope for light. Every year people in Boston keep asking why Jim Rice is paid a salary in excess of two million dollars, as he strikes out inning after inning. Just as they are in despair – Rice is in despair too, but does not show it – he pulls the cat out of the bag, goes on a hitting streak, drives in home runs and wins whole successions of games almost single handed.

Reggie Jackson was another who went into a notoriously bad slump and forced New York supporters to ask why he had been brought from the west, and why for three million

139

dollars. He had helped Oakland win the World Series three times, but the transition east just did not seem to be working. He hit adequately during the season, but no more than that. He argued in public with the effusive Yankees' manager, Billy Martin. Jackson is a difficult, complex man and all his problems seemed to be coming home to roost, as they sometimes do with baseball stars thrust far into the limelight. During the play-offs in the American League he had only two hits during fifteen times at bat. In the first two games of the World Series he had only one single in six times at bat. Was this man worth all the trouble and the brouha-ha?

He was. In the fourth game he hit a double and then two home runs. In the fifth game in his first time at bat he was walked – deliberate walking of star hitters happens quite often in the World Series. Then he hit a home run, first ball. His next time on deck he hit another home run, first ball. Then he did it again. The last four home runs had all been on the first pitch, one in the fourth game, three in the fifth. It is said to have been the greatest single batting performance ever delivered over a short period of time. And he had been in the doldrums just before.

A similar great moment, a similar great return, was that of Willie Mays to New York. An astonishing hitter with six hundred and sixty home runs, third behind Aaron and Ruth, Mays, who came from deep in Alabama, was also a fielder who made the sometimes routine position of centre field come alive. His most famous moment occurred when playing for the New York Giants in the 1954 World Series, against Cleveland. It was only Cleveland's second appearance in the series, and the first for over three decades. In a position where they looked like clinching the winning game, they already had two men on base. Then one Vic Wertz smashed the ball into centre field, the deepest part of the park, a ball that would have been a home run if hit on another angle. Fielders are known to run back astonishing distances against high balls, but this was hit hard on a low angle. Astonishingly Mays ran

140

back, caught the ball back-handed while still running, then threw it to the infield to prevent the runners moving. It is said to have been among the greatest catches of all time, and from then on the New York Giants were able to turn the tables on Cleveland. The catch had in fact only been bettered by another astonishing catch by Mays himself, made two years before when in a similar situation, and playing the Brooklyn Dodgers, he flung himself against the wall, caught a driving ball and was knocked unconscious, the umpire having to come out not to diagnose the patient, but to decide whether the ball, under Mays' body, was still in his gloved hand and above the turf. It was.

Mays was also a great hitter, his greatest feat being performed on the day when, suffering from a bad stomach and dubious about playing he slugged four home runs off Milwaukee, four in five times at bat, four times in a nine inning game, something only eight other players had achieved since the turn of the century. Shortly after this Mays left New York for fourteen long years, only to be re-acquired at the age of forty-one by the new New York Mets, a team that originated in 1962, ingloriously won only forty out of a hundred and sixty games in that first season, but seven years later won their first World Series. It was three years after this that Mays came back, to New York scepticism mixed with joy at the return of a boy wonder, now an old man. The first two games he sat on the bench. In the third he had his chance. In his first time at bat he walked. In his second the score against Montreal was four all. Mays hit the home run that won the game. In a sense, it was just another game in another season. But, in the baseball memories and minds of those who knew, it was much more – much, much more.

APPENDIX 1

NINETEEN EASY STEPS TO ENJOYING BASEBALL

1 Be patient. Baseball evolved from a puritan ethic: the best things in life do not come easily.
2 Watch the pitcher as much as the hitter. Don't expect to get satisfaction out of the big hits alone. Home runs come less often than goals in a football match. Confusing home runs with what is really going on in baseball is a bit like orgasm and love. One needs the other.
3 Remember that fundamentally baseball is a game of individuals as much as of teams. The key individuals are the pitcher and the man at bat.
4 Remember that each individual has a limited number of chances. Four wide 'balls' and the batter walks to first base. He can let two straight pitches past him as 'strikes'. But after two strikes against him he has to hit the ball. If he is caught he is out, if he is run out he is out, if he misses the third straight pitch he is out on strikes.
5 Keep a mental tally of the count. Balls go first, strikes second. So

that 2 and 1 means two balls, one strike, meaning the hitter has a more than even chance. 2 and 2 means two balls, two strikes meaning that the hitter has to do something soon.

6   Identify the order of hitting. Write it down if shown on television. If you remember that steady hitters are at the top, big hitters, the clean-up men, in the middle and the weak at the bottom of the order you will begin to anticipate and predict the action.

7   Identify the pattern of the pitcher's work. Is he throwing fast and striking everyone out? Can you expect him to go on like that? If he is being hit, why is he being hit?

8   Look at the men on base. Are they trying to steal?

9   Look at the fielders. Are they close in or far out? Are the first and second basemen having to hold down men who are trying to steal, thereby leaving gaps?

10 Don't look for home runs – that is rather like looking for fivers on the street. Look at the way a person hits, and note it from inning to inning. Some lead-off hitters do not hit the ball very hard. They place it, one of the baseball's great arts.

11 Try and understand the factors that make baseball such a close game: the distance between the bases, and the limited chances of hitter and pitcher.

12 Don't just look at the runs scored. Look at the number of people stranded on base as well.

13 Read about and around baseball; don't just study the rules.

14 Remember that excerpted baseball on television is not the real thing. At best the camera shows less than the eye sees (although it may reveal extra detail), and editors will go for what they consider highlights, the hits. For my money non-hits can be just as interesting; when you are watching non-hits you are watching great pitching.

15 Watch or play amateur baseball, in a park or on a beach. You can make your own rules for pitching, e.g. throwing underhand, set your own boundaries and put the bases far enough apart to make them difficult but not impossible to reach. Use a cricket bat and tennis ball.

16 If you are serious, join a baseball league. Details about them can be obtained from The Sports Council, 16 Upper Woburn Place, London WC1.

17 If you are really serious, go to a baseball game in the US. Afternoon games are easier to get into than night games, but night games have more atmosphere. Baseball is always safe for children; violence is rare, and soccer type violence almost unknown. Buy the most expensive seats you can. There is only about three dollars' difference between the cheap and the expensive, and the view from behind home plate or first or third base gives more symmetry to the game when you do not fully understand it.

18 Always remember that baseball, like beer, is an acquired taste. Americans get blasé about baseball sometimes, but those who watch and read always come back for more.

19 Talk to Americans about baseball. Some will be outside the game, but even then you can learn something. It will have figured somewhere in their lives, even if they did not like the experience, never quite made it, or supported a team that went phut.

APPENDIX 2

BASEBALL AND CRICKET: SIMILARITIES AND DISSIMILARITIES

SIMILARITIES

1 Both are played with a stick and ball.
2 Both have their origins way back in history, stick and ball games having for centuries been played either in a straight line (on a wicket), or in the round (on a diamond).
3 In both you score by running.
4 In both you can be caught out.
5 Both have boundary lines, and hits that go beyond the boundary score high (four or six in cricket, a home run in baseball).
6 Both have an infield and outfield. In cricket the fielding side, including bowlers numbers eleven. In baseball it numbers nine.
7 Both pitcher and bowler must be within certain limits before projecting the ball.
8 Both games have strict rules about the manner and action whereby the ball is projected.
9 In both games fielding strategy, designed to support pitchers/bowlers and to hamper hitters/batsmen, is crucial. The tactics

are very different, partly because in baseball it is necessary for three fielders to defend the bases, and partly because of the different shapes of cricket field and baseball park.

10 In both games the man behind the aiming point (catcher or wicket keeper) has a crucial task.

11 In both games there is the concept of the inning or innings.

12 In both games occur the similar concepts of the 'bye' and the 'error'.

13 The wicket and the plate are more similar as targets than may appear at first sight, given the concept of a ball going through the strike zone, and that of lbw, where the umpire judges whether the ball might have hit the wicket.

14 The concept of the batter's box and of the crease are similar. A batter may not leave the box. A batsman who leaves the crease does so at the risk of being stumped.

15 Most important, appreciation of both games depends more on a spectator's knowledge of tactics and player performance, than on the spectacle *per se*.

DISSIMILARITIES

1 In baseball there can be no draw, and there is much less defensive play.

2 In cricket a side can force a draw to prevent a win.

3 In general the pitcher is on top in baseball.

4 Runs come more frequently in cricket, and the game usually lasts longer. In baseball twenty hits is a lot for one side batting for half the time of a three and a half hour game. At an equivalent nine runs an hour cricket would soon lose all popularity.

5 Outs come more frequently in baseball. Fifty-four outs in three and a half hours is about nine an hour. That would be pretty fast cricket.

6 In baseball there is only one point to aim for by the pitcher, only one home plate. In cricket there are two – two sets of stumps, two alternating bowlers.

7 Once taken out of the game, a pitcher cannot return to it.

8 Boundary lines in baseball restrict the angle of fair hits around the man at bat to 90°. The cricket equivalent is 360°.

9 In cricket one straight ball missed is out; bowled, or leg before wicket, if it satisfies the complex l.b.w. rules. In baseball the man at bat is out on the third straight pitch, *but* has few defensive opportunities, whereas the batsman in cricket has many.

10 In baseball, to pass through the strike zone the ball must not hit the ground. One which does is automatically counted against the pitcher as a 'ball'.

11 'Wides' exists in both games, but are differently defined.

12 In baseball a run only counts when the man has rounded all the bases.

13 In baseball it is compulsory to run when the ball is hit into fair territory. In cricket all running is voluntary. As a result running out is far more common in baseball.

14 Baseball is less affected by the weather than cricket.

15 Baseball has no equivalent to the 'over', a fixed number of balls to be bowled by one person at one time.

16 Baseball has no real equivalent to being 'not out', although hitters are judged on the number of hits rather than on the number of runs they score. Thus hitters left stranded at bases are not penalized in their averages.

APPENDIX 3

FURTHER READING

Baseball books are hard to find in Britain. But if you go to the Sportspages book shop which is just off Charing Cross Road in London you will find a remarkably large number.

You can buy the rules, published by the Sporting News; there is a selection of statistical books, including the Macmillian Encyclopaedia of Baseball, which Americans consider the best ever produced, by the time this book is published they hope to stock Bill James' wry but invaluable Historical Baseball Abstract.

There is a good selection of other titles, some in paperback, the holding expanding all the time.

For background reading, if you can obtain them, books published in the Penguin Sports Library are almost all worth reading. 'The Boys of Summer', an account of the post World War II Brooklyn Dodgers, by Roger Kahn, is considered by some one of the best books on the sport. It is written in a novelish style and, like many such books, uses a good deal of baseball language. 'The Summer Game', by Roger Angell, is a series of essays by a fluent writer whose love of baseball pours onto the page. The best compressed guide is the Access Guide. Access specializes in guides to American cities, but I find their one on baseball an incredible exercise in compression.

The literature of baseball is huge and new titles keep appearing. If you cannot find titles at the Sports Bookcentre in London, all US bookshops have a large selection. So does the Baseball Hall of Fame, although it tends to the more expensive hardbacks.

For information on baseball leagues in Britain, Sportspages is again a useful source. So is the Sports Council.

For scores, the Daily Telegrapah is the best British source. Otherwise you have to buy USA Today (outrageously expensive in Britain), or the Herald Tribune. Instructions on learning how to score can be found in the front of score books.

INDEX TO TERMS
AND
DEFINITIONS

151